1. Use a planner and take it everywhere.

2. Delegate as many unpleasant or time-consuming tasks as possible.

3. Get your world organized—at home and at the office.

4. Make appointments with yourself to have fun.

5. Learn to say "no."

One luxurious
bubble bath

Access to most comfortable
chair and favorite TV show

One half-hour massage
(will need to recruit spouse, child, friend)

Time to recline and listen to a favorite CD
(or at least one song)

Do it

The Lazy Way

6. Take care of yourself with enough rest, exercise, and proper nutrition.

7. Make a short list of goals.

8. Cut way back on TV-watching.

9. Accept the fact that you can't do it all.

10. Keep a positive attitude.

COUPON

COUPON

COUPON

COUPON

Manage
Your
Time

The Lazy Way™

Manage Your Time

Toni Ahlgren

Macmillan • USA

To the three most important men in my life; my sons, Niklas, Douglas, and Thomas. I am so proud of you guys; I hope this makes you proud of your mom.

Macmillan Publishing books may be purchased for business or sales promotional use. For information please write: Special Markets Department, Macmillan Publishing USA, 1633 Broadway, New York, NY 10019.

International Standard Book Number: 0-02-863169-2
Library of Congress Catalog Card Number available upon request.

01 00 99   8 7 6 5 4 3 2 1

Interpretation of the printing code: the rightmost number of the first series of numbers is the year of the book's printing; the rightmost number of the second series of numbers is the number of the book's printing. For example, a printing code of 99-1 shows that the first printing occurred in 1999.

Printed in the United States of America

Book Design: Madhouse Studios

Page Creation: Heather Pope

You Don't Have to Feel Guilty Anymore!

IT'S O.K. TO DO IT *THE LAZY WAY!*

It seems every time we turn around, we're given more responsibility, more information to absorb, more places we need to go, and more numbers, dates, and names to remember. Both our bodies and our minds are already on overload. And we know what happens next—cleaning the house, balancing the checkbook, and cooking dinner get put off until "tomorrow" and eventually fall by the wayside.

So let's be frank—we're all starting to feel a bit guilty about the dirty laundry, stacks of ATM slips, and Chinese takeout. Just thinking about tackling those terrible tasks makes you exhausted, right? If only there were an easy, effortless way to get this stuff done! (And done right!)

There is—*The Lazy Way*! By providing the pain-free way to do something—including tons of shortcuts and timesaving tips, as well as lists of all the stuff you'll ever need to get it done efficiently—*The Lazy Way* series cuts through all of the time-wasting thought processes and laborious exercises. You'll discover the secrets of those who have figured out *The Lazy Way*. You'll get things done in half the time it takes the average person—and then you will sit back and smugly consider those poor suckers who haven't discovered *The Lazy Way* yet. With *The Lazy Way,* you'll learn how to put in minimal effort and get maximum results so you can devote your attention and energy to the pleasures in life!

THE LAZY WAY PROMISE

Everyone on *The Lazy Way* staff promises that, if you adopt *The Lazy Way* philosophy, you'll never break a sweat, you'll barely lift a finger, you won't put strain on your brain, and you'll have plenty of time to put up your feet. We guarantee you will find that these activities are no longer hardships, since you're doing them *The Lazy Way*. We also firmly support taking breaks and encourage rewarding yourself (we even offer our suggestions in each book!). With *The Lazy Way*, the only thing you'll be overwhelmed by is all of your newfound free time!

THE LAZY WAY SPECIAL FEATURES

Every book in our series features the following sidebars in the margins, all designed to save you time and aggravation down the road.

- **"Quick 'n' Painless"**—shortcuts that get the job done fast.

- **"You'll Thank Yourself Later"**—advice that saves time down the road.

- **"A Complete Waste of Time"**—warnings that spare countless headaches and squandered hours.

- **"If You're So Inclined"**—optional tips for moments of inspired added effort.

- **"The Lazy Way"**—rewards to make the task more pleasurable.

If you've either decided to give up altogether or have taken a strong interest in the subject, you'll find information on hiring outside help with "How to Get Someone Else to Do It" as well as further reading recommendations in "If You Really Want More, Read These." In addition, there's an only-what-you-need-to-know glossary of terms and product names ("If You Don't Know What It Means/Does, Look Here") as well as "It's Time for Your Reward"—fun and relaxing ways to treat yourself for a job well done.

With *The Lazy Way* series, you'll find that getting the job done has never been so painless!

Series Editor
Amy Gordon

Cover Designer
Michael J. Freeland

Editorial Director
Gary M. Krebs

Managing Editor
Robert Shuman

Development Editor
Alana Morgan

Director of Creative Services
Michele Laseau

Production Editor
Scott Barnes

What's in This Book

How Did We All Get So Busy and What to Do About It

"Where does the time go?" is often more than a flip phrase expressed as a child celebrates yet another birthday on the heels of the last one, or you finally get around to looking for a bathing suit—only to find that the stores are already decorated for Thanksgiving. Truly scary!

Have hope. This book should arm you with ideas to help slow down the clock. There are a slew of quick, *Lazy Way* fixes for everyone from stay-at-home moms to traveling executives. The real key to effective time management takes, for all of us, a bit of thought: thought spent on figuring out your priorities, your interests, your lifestyle, and your personal and professional goals—all within the fixed parameters of your life. Clearly defining your goals will help you sweep your path clean of the less important jumble of activities and commitments you're stumbling over.

Let me assure you that getting your goals established isn't always easy. If it were, all of us would have our goal lists neatly typed out in front of us, waiting for their yearly updates. But don't worry: The time you'll spend to get organized will pay off! I guarantee that you'll enjoy the journey from scattered to serene and the transition from frantic to finished.

You're a step ahead of the game just reading this book. Take on the challenge and enjoy your trip.

THE SPECIAL THANKS

Many thanks to my dear friends who supported me—in many ways—during the evolution of this book: my clients, who managed interruptions in their care; my able assistants, Debbie Vogel and Sabrina Keller, who came to the fore, took up the slack, and showed enormous flexibility and competence; my delightful Doncaster ladies, who might have gotten less than 110 percent from me the last few months; Mary Kay Fry, who fed and housed me and created a wonderful space so I could write; and Karen Miller, Connie Cox, Julie Ann Kodmur, Barbara Bernadette, Candi Czapleski, Ginna Bell Bragg, Kathy Bertolino, and countless other buddies who have cheered me on every step of the way.

On the publishing side of my team, thank you to Martha Casselman, for being super-agent, to Amy Gordon in the skyscraper in New York, who let me do my thing, and to Alana Morgan, who has acted as my personal coach, cheerleading section, and midwife, month by month, chapter by chapter.

Part 1

The Bits and Pieces That Will Keep You Together

Are You Too Lazy to Read "The Bits and Pieces That Will Keep You Together"?

1 *Sure* you can get your hands on your kids' Social Security numbers. They have to be here *somewhere*, don't they? ☐ yes ☐ no

2 Sleep is that thing you only have time to do when you're on an airplane. ☐ yes ☐ no

3 You just know that those computer manuals that you got in 1982 are going to be museum-worthy some day. ☐ yes ☐ no

one

Little Things to Keep You Moving

Get set to pull together the tricks of the trade and the basics to help you keep your life on track and give yourself some breathing room. Remember: One of the foundations of efficient time management is being organized. I discuss how to do just that later in the book, but like anyone who is about to embark on a project, you need to make sure that you have the right stuff to do the job.

A real time-saver is to buy in bulk and keep a good inventory of supplies on hand. Yes, you'll need room in which to store extras, but running out of envelopes in the middle of a mailing, computer disks while backing up your computer files, or clean sheets on bed-changing day can create a mild crisis and an ill-timed shopping trip—at the very least!

Following is a list of things you might need to help the time-management process along. Don't be dismayed; you won't need all of these items, but a few will certainly keep you working at a speedier rate in the future. Later, I discuss how to use these items most efficiently.

Take inventory of your house and office before you go out and spend a fortune on new supplies. You might find once everything is collected that you have enough goodies to keep you in business for a year.

When you decide on a particular area of your life that you want to streamline, these lists of basic supplies will act as a good memory jogger.

HELPING THE HOUSE HELP YOU

Here are some general goodies for around the house, some of which you'll wonder how you ever lived without. Other suggestions might be new ways for you to use familiar items.

Hooks, Hooks, and More Hooks

One of the basic rules of organizing is to get things off the floor. Hooks are defense weapon number one in that battle. A hook gives you a better alternative than the floor for your clothes, while also keeping them slightly less wrinkled than draping them all over the furniture. Besides, fewer wrinkled clothes means less laundry!

Wet towels dry better when hung on a hook rather than dropped in piles, staying wet, which just necessitates a new towel—and more laundry.

Kids' toys are a great candidate for mesh bags on hooks: They'll be visible and accessible but won't clutter the floor.

Hooks also work wonderfully for bathroom toys and sponges; they'll drain themselves dry if you keep them in mesh bags hung from the shower head. Once they've drip-dried, just remove the bags from the shower—unless you prefer the company of rubber duckies!—and hang them on hooks that you've installed on the bathroom walls or in a closet.

Mud rooms, foyers, entry ways—all these areas could benefit from hooks for everything from jackets to jump ropes to hats. Just make sure you place hooks at the proper height for little people. Of course, it might take some training to get all family members to use these wonderful hooks, but with time, everyone will eventually get the idea … really!

Shelves, Shelves, and More Shelves

Weapon number two for keeping clutter to a minimum and finding more space are shelves—"climbing the walls" is the key phrase here! In the office, shelves give you linear yards of more storage space to house binders, books, research materials, photographs, your Grammy Award or Nobel Prize, a few *objets d'art*, manuals, supplies, and whatever else seems to gravitate to the office.

Bedrooms are another great spot for shelves, but believe it or not, they're not often used there. Books and photographs that normally clutter a nightstand are obvious choices for bedroom shelves, but why not hobby materials, photograph albums, or your collection of stuffed African lizards?

Your music equipment—now that some components are the size of postage stamps—can also fit on shelves, so that you no longer require those bulky entertainment centers of the 80s.

Children's bedrooms can never have too many shelves for all their collections of books, Barbie stuff, games, and tiny plastic treasures.

IF YOU'RE SO INCLINED

Stumped with a lack of long, flat wall space? Check out the wide variety of corner shelving that is available to help you out!

The garage could always use another shelf or two. Even with diligent purging, we all need extra room sometimes—if for no other reason than to store old tax returns and the like. Shelves in the garage—placed high above dampness and dust—could be the answer.

In the laundry room, an extra shelf will hold a bin of rags or cleaning supplies or the case of toilet paper you bought on sale. If you're not lucky enough to have a pantry, you can improvise one by installing shelves in either the laundry room or the garage, giving you oodles more space for canned goods, jars, and boxes.

Second Hanging Rods in Closets

I'm trying to think of anyone I've ever met during my professional organizing career who thought she had enough closet space. Personally, I think there must be a natural law that the scientists just haven't discovered yet that says that no matter how much closet space you have, it will still be inadequate for your needs.

If you find yourself running short—even after you've thrown out or removed what you could from your closets—consider hanging a second closet rod below the existing one. You will double the space you have to hang "short" stuff—blouses, shirts, and slacks folded in half. You'll find kits to do this easily at home stores and department stores that sell organizing supplies. Even though these closet rods might be called "children's closet rods" (apparently designed originally to help kids hang up their own clothes) they'll work just as well in your own closet.

QUICK ⊂⊃ PAINLESS

When storing groups of little things on shelves, be sure they're encased in a practical and attractive container. For example, you can put magazines into magazine butlers, your makeup into baskets, toys into plastic bins, and your shells into big glass jars. Keeping collections housed together will make it easy to access them, will make it easier to dust the shelf, and will keep your belongings out of sight—or attractively displayed—and dust free to boot!

Recycling Bins

Finding a place to put recycling and getting the right equipment for the job will make it a lot easier to see that it gets done at your house. Don't forget to recycle at the office—a tremendous generator of waste. Set up a place with the correct bins and containers to make the job easy.

Each community has its own rules, services, and limitations, so what works for me won't necessarily apply in your hometown. Call your local disposal company to determine what it'll recycle and what containers are appropriate.

Storage Bins

Bins come in just about any configuration you can imagine. The most useful are rectangular ones, somewhat see-through with lids. "Containerize" your out-of-season clothes, rock collections, tax returns, accessories, dress-up costumes, shoes, gardening supplies, hobby and craft equipment, memorabilia, memo pads, pencils and erasers, and building blocks.

You'll find plastic bins everywhere; some are designed especially to hold particular items, whereas others are multipurpose. The bins made to accommodate file folders are extremely useful for long-term storage of important documents because they keep the dust and moisture at bay.

Plastic bins range in size from as small as a salt shaker to jumbo boxes that are designed to hold blankets and pillows. The good ones might not be cheap, but they are well worth the investment.

Congratulations! You've found a way to help cut down on waste generation! Do a little personal recycling and revisit a favorite book!

The Lazy Way

Take advantage of all the different shapes and sizes of plastic containers on the market. Not only will they keep things neat, but you'll be cutting down on finding spoiled food in your kitchen, too!

In the kitchen, you can maintain order by depositing your dried foods into containers made especially for food. If your kitchen is prone to attracting little flying creatures, you'll find you have less of them in your space by containing your food packages.

For example, I put all my bags of rice into containers with tight lids. (I don't bother emptying the bags, however; I just shove the whole thing right into the container.) When my household used to go through a lot of dried cereal, I poured the contents of the boxes into Rubbermaid's cereal containers; they made it easier for my boys to get their own breakfast, and it was easier for me to keep an eye on how much was left.

Baskets

I think baskets are better looking than plastic bins, but unfortunately, they generally aren't as durable. Use them for storing things where aesthetics are important.

Here's an idea to try: Hide your office supplies from view in attractive square baskets neatly lined up along a shelf in your office.

In the kitchen, you can keep the blades to the food processor safely out of the way in a good-looking basket.

The things that emerge from your pockets at the end of the day—loose change, matchbook, and credit card receipts, for example—can be neatly housed in a basket, rather than spread all over the top of your dresser.

I've always had a basket on my vanity to hold bathroom supplies I use every day. This technique makes wiping the counter-top easy: You just lift the basket and get all the stuff out of the way at once. Using a basket can also be a good warning system. If your counter is littered with more bottles and jars than you can fit into your basket, you'll know it's time to pare down or put things away.

Drawer Dividers

Great for a lot more than just utensils in the kitchen drawers, drawer dividers can be used to organize small office supplies in a drawer, hardware in the garage, hobby supplies, electric cords, makeup and skin-care products, jewelry, socks, and sewing notions. You can gain valuable space by stacking two dividers on top of each other. Often called utensil trays, they come in a variety of materials, such as plastic, rattan, and metal.

It's also a good idea to be on the look-out for interlocking boxes—usually made of plastic—that you can buy in different sizes to fit your drawers and their contents exactly.

Pegboards and Bulletin Boards

Pegboards are great for the same reason hooks are great; they get stuff off counters and floors. Mostly used in garages on which to hang tools, pegboards can also be handy in the kitchen to hang utensils and small pots and pans. I've also seen them used in kids' rooms to keep hangable toys and clothes in order.

If you really want to impress your friends and neighbors, outline the items you hang on your pegboard with a wide marking pen. That way, you'll always know where

QUICK 🔲 *PAINLESS*

Install a pegboard in the kitchen for your pots and pans and they'll always be handy!

your tools should go when you're done with them, and you'll also know whether something got borrowed by the kids.

You should use bulletin boards with restraint because they tend to fill up. Less delicately put, bulletin boards can look like hell with tons of papers crammed into a limited space. I'm talking about everything from outdated memos—faded with time—and tattered scraps of paper dangling from push-pins. What an eyesore!

A bulletin board is just not the place to display "the layered look," but it is handy for posting notes that everyone at the office or home needs to see and to keep frequently used information in front of your nose in your workspace. The big thing to remember here is to keep your bulletin board neat. Edit it often!

Another nifty tool is something made by Abbott Office Systems. Its "organizers" are basically binders, propped up on a tilted stand (for good visibility) and filled with plastic sheet protectors into which you can slide frequently referenced information. You can place them on your desktop, above it on a movable arm, or attached to a wall close to your desk. They're a wonderful alternative to messy bulletin boards, files, or papers scattered all over your workspace.

Buckets and Boxes for Toys

I mentioned plastic bins earlier; keep an eye out for buckets with lids. I always had my boys' Legos stored in a bucket, which makes them easy to move around. If floor space is limited, use boxes that can be stacked.

IF YOU'RE SO INCLINED

Keep your bulletin board limited to holding pertinent phone numbers and you can breathe easy that your family will be able to handle any emergency without wasting valuable time sifting through useless memos!

Duvet Covers

I swear by duvet covers, the large "envelopes" into which you put a comforter or blanket. They come in a wide variety of colors and patterns and in every bed size. A duvet cover replaces a top sheet, the blanket, and a bedspread. By changing covers, you can change the decor of your bedroom almost instantaneously. Bed-making is a snap: Just shake out the "envelope" and smooth it down.

Plastic Baskets

I'm referring here to open baskets in a general-purpose size of approximately 10" to 15". These are handy to put in the cupboards under the bathroom sink for general supplies, hair products, and skin products. You can simply remove the whole basket and place it on the counter to find something or to clean the bottom of the cupboard.

These baskets are also handy—in smaller sizes—to hold hair accessories, band aids and gauze boxes, and other similar first-aid supplies. Small baskets also work well in kitchen cupboards; they can hold soup and sauce envelopes, tea bags, or your collection of bouillon cubes.

Zip-Locking Plastic Bags

Take a bunch of these along when you travel; they're good for packing anything that could break or leak, grouping like items together (such as socks or pantyhose), storing dirty laundry, and keeping together rolls of film or the collection of shells you gathered on the beach.

Plastic bags are also great for storing kids' tiny things: Barbie shoes, beads, puzzle pieces, or a lovely

A COMPLETE WASTE OF TIME

The 3 Worst Things You Can Do with Your Bedroom Are:

1. Fail to use duvet covers.

2. Litter miscellaneous stuff on every surface.

3. Fail to use baskets and attractive containers for storage.

rock collection. I love the tiny Zip Lock bags; they measure only 6$\frac{1}{2}$" by 3$\frac{1}{4}$" and they're called "snack bags." They're terrific for pills, buttons, candy, Barbie shoes, seeds, game pieces, and coupons.

Laundry Hampers

Keep plenty of these around in households with children. One in each bathroom and each bedroom is not overkill. You can stash them out of sight perhaps—in the closets or even under the sink. Woven hampers look great, but be sure their interior surface is smooth; rough ones can snag your clothes badly.

Mesh Bags

I've mentioned these as great bathroom helpers, to hold wet bath toys up and out of the way. Mesh bags can also be a great boon while traveling to hold like things together. Of course, you can skip hand-washing nylons and delicates by putting them into mesh bags and tossing them into the washing machine.

Bankers Boxes

Banker's boxes are generally made of cardboard and hold paper manila folders in either legal or letter size. They have lids and you buy them flat. They easily fold up into sturdy boxes that stack easily, useful for long-term storage. Use banker's boxes in dry areas; because they're paper, too much moisture is not the ideal storage environment for them.

I buy mine in bulk from Quill because I tend to use them for more than just storage. They're easily transportable, and because they have cut-out hand grips, they make it easy to cart things around. I've put one on the floor under my desk to collect tax information at the beginning of the year and have used them to hold bulky materials for a short-term project. They're also a good, stable way to transport stuff in the car, such as the casserole due at the potluck dinner.

MAKING YOUR OFFICE OPERATIONAL

Here are some office supplies that you'll be able to use both at the office and at home:

- **Paper planner/organizer.** I discuss using a planner in Chapter 8, "Using a Planner," so if you don't already own one, be sure to read that chapter before you rush out to purchase one.

- **Office utensils.** Gather your favorite pens, pencils, permanent markers, sticky notes, stapler, staple remover. These items should be well organized in a handy drawer if you have one. If not, place them into baskets on a nearby shelf.

- **Permanent markers.** I find these best for mailing labels (they don't wash away in rainy weather) and for writing big, bold folder headings.

- **Dividers.** Meant to hold frequently used file folders upright, these dividers are usually made of metal or plastic and are great to use for keeping frequently needed files on your desktop without losing too much workspace. I like the add-on type—Eldon's Add-A-File especially—because they're made of

YOU'LL THANK YOURSELF LATER

Buy the best file cabinet you can afford. Cheap ones just will not hold up! Their drawers often fall off their tracks or become hard to open and close, generally making filing a real pain. You want to make this chore as easy as possible.

interlocking pieces; you can use as many—or as few—as you need. Because they simply snap together, you can adjust the number of files you store on your desktop in a flash. In Chapter 9, "Time-Savers at the Office," I walk you through setting up and using a system with these dividers.

- **Paper goods.** You need a supply of envelopes, letterhead, note pads, shipping labels, postage stamps, padded envelopes, and fax paper. By keeping these supplies together, you create a system—the best way to save time. Should you need to jot a quick note to someone or pack a box, you want all your supplies handy, accessible, and appropriate for the job so you can accomplish it in no time flat. The idea behind getting organized like this is to prevent you from spending any time at all wandering around, looking for supplies.

- **Calculator.** I know it's good for your brain cells to do the math, but you want to manage your time, right? Get an adding machine or calculator. That suggestion applies at home, too.

- **Rubber stamps.** I discuss this in more detail later, but just think for a moment of all the things you find yourself writing by hand over and over again every day, every week. If you obtain a few strategically thought-out rubber stamps, you could save countless hours and never subject yourself to cramping hands again.

- **Banking supplies.** Assembling such supplies as checks, deposit slips, and bank-by-mail envelopes

QUICK 🐷 PAINLESS

Pre-printed return address labels will make sending correspondence and bills a snap! Give it a try!

will create another system for bill-paying and making deposits. If they don't fit into a drawer, put them into a basket that you can pull out when it's banking and bill-paying time. Having everything together might make the task a little less onerous. At the very least, being organized about bills and finances will have you spending less time on those tasks.

- **Batteries.** Make sure you have extra batteries for anything in your home or office that requires them. There's nothing more frustrating than being stopped in your tracks by a tiny battery that has no more to give you. Compound that with the time spent looking for a replacement battery—and not finding one—and you've got the formula for major time-wasting! I keep mine in a small plastic bin along with a simple, inexpensive battery tester from Radio Shack. That tester saved me a lot of guesswork when my boys had a fleet of battery-operated vehicles careening around the house.

- **Desk.** I know this seems obvious, but you'd be surprised! You can use anything from a card table to a corner of the kitchen counter to a teak monolith meant for showoffs. The point here is to get a desk area that you use for everything you do that involves paper.

- **A good chair.** The emphasis here is on *good*. Buy the best you can afford. Your back, neck, and shoulders will thank you for it, and your productivity will soar!

- **File cabinet**. From a roomful to a desktop box—your needs will vary, of course, depending upon what you do and how much paper you're blessed (or cursed) with. Even at home, you need the equivalent of a file cabinet to manage paperwork efficiently. You can find them in two-drawer to five-drawer models, regular or lateral, in a variety of colors, finishes, and quality standards. There's a file cabinet out there to fit your size needs as well as aesthetic requirements.

- **Hanging folders.** Pendaflex is the standard bearer for hanging folders; they're the dark green ones with hooks on either side that hang on rods in the file drawer. Hanging folders make getting around a file drawer fast work because they slide back and forth easily. You don't remove a hanging folder: It sits there waiting to hold a paper folder. You can get them in great colors now, making it easier to color-code a filing system. (Or you just might be mad for teal folders.)

- **Manila folders.** If you get the ones that are third cut, that means the tabs are big—which means you can print bold names that will be easy to see. Visibility is crucial to speeding up the filing process; the better you can see your files, the faster you'll go. These folders are the workhorse of a filing system. They also come in colors, in colored or clear plastic, and in regular or heavy-duty versions. These options are great for those of you who hope to graduate to a highly evolved filing system.

- **Wastepaper basket.** You can never have too many of these babies: close by the mail's point of entry, in kids' rooms, by every desk, in the garage, and in the laundry room to catch pocket and laundering debris.

- **Bookcases or shelves**. Get as many as can fit into your space. See the section "Helping the House Help You," earlier in the chapter. Bookcases needn't cost a lot. You'll find them new or used, for general home or specific office purposes, painted or natural, in stores or garage sales. Of course, you can always have beautiful built-ins installed if you have the budget. A handy person can help with shelves, which can range in style and price from fine cabinetry to fiber boards on metal brackets.

- **Telephone headset.** Even at home, if you spend hours on the phone, a headset is a head saver. Read about telephone headsets in Chapter 9.

- **Good lighting.** Good visibility is the key to efficient work. All desks should have a "task light" to illuminate the work at hand. Good reading lamps are crucial and might even result in more reading at your house; see that there are good lamps by the bedside, by the couch or armchair, and in children's rooms. Overhead lights generally cast an unflattering, harsh light; avoid them unless they can be put on a dimmer. Whenever possible, to save floor and or table space, see if you can install wall-mounted lighting fixtures.

- **Bankers boxes.** These are essential at the office and for long-term storage where moisture isn't a

YOU'LL THANK YOURSELF LATER

If you spend a lot of your day on the phone, treat yourself to a phone headset so life doesn't come to a halt every time the phone rings.

If you seem to need duplicate supplies (wastebaskets, for example) it's not indulgent of you to get them. If you regularly deal with the kids' school papers at the kitchen table instead of your office, then it might make sense to have a second stapler and scissors in the kitchen. It's a big time-waster to frequently wander from room to room to finish a chore, so buy supplies for all the places you frequently use them.

problem. Read why in the section "Helping the House Help You," earlier in the chapter.

- **Stamps.** Along with mailing supplies and the postage meter or scale, you'll have a mailing system in place if you have a variety of stamps in different denominations on hand.

- **Postage scale (or meter).** Particularly if you do a lot of mailings, this is a time- and money-saver that can't be beat.

- **Address book or Rolodex.** Whether it's electronic or paper, you *must* have one place to collect all the names and numbers that come into your life. Learn how to make the most of an address book in Chapter 3, "Getting the Ball Rolling."

KEEPING YOUR KITCHEN UNDER CONTROL

Some of these items are for saving space, and others will help by increasing visibility of the things you need to store in kitchen cupboards and shelves. I figure that if you can see it, you won't waste time rummaging around looking for it:

- **Cup hooks.** These will keep cups and mugs visible and save cupboard space as well.

- **Baskets for counter-top collecting.** Use a basket to hold the vitamin bottles or the pens, pencils, and message pads. Containers control clutter!

- **Turntables for cupboards.** Rubbermaid makes "lazy Susans" that revolve, making whatever's in back visible in front. They come in a range of sizes to accommodate spice jars or pots and pans. See if they don't solve some of your storage problems.

- **Drawer dividers**. Whether in plastic, wire, or rattan, these are great little helpers behind the scenes.

- **Wine rack.** If you like wine, then treat it—and yourself—well. A good wine rack will save you space, and protect your investment by storing it properly. Wine is best stored out of the kitchen where temperatures can fluctuate significantly. Look around for a cool spot elsewhere in your home for better wine storage—and you'll free up some kitchen space at the same time!

- **Bulletin board.** Just keep it updated and neat, and it will speak for itself.

- **Family organizing calendar.** Basically, make a place for family members to stay in the know about everyone else's plans. See Chapter 11, "Fitting Family Life into the Puzzle."

- **Wire racks to hold canned goods.** Step-like racks hold a back row of jars or cans higher than the front row so you can see everything at a glance; it makes for speedy retrieval.

- **Hooks.** Use these to keep brooms, mops, dishtowels, and hot pads handy. Using hooks follows the philosophy of getting things up and on the walls. In the kitchen, you'll save yourself drawer and counter space by hanging what you can. Don't forget the option of getting your pots and pans (at least the pretty ones) hanging from a pot rack.

QUICK ◼ PAINLESS

Use a dry-erase calendar board! They're easy to clean and the changing schedules of a hectic family will still be neat and clear! (Look ma! No scratch outs!)

UTILIZING YOUR UTILITY AREAS: THE GARAGE AND LAUNDRY ROOM

These two rooms have been likened to the Bermuda Triangle: Belongings just seem to disappear once they get in the vicinity. Some of the following items will help keep your stuff in circulation:

- Recycling bins—see if your disposal company provides these. If it doesn't, look for stackable ones to save room.
- Pegboards on which to hang tools.
- Clothesline.
- Shelving units.
- Smooth plastic tubular hangers.
- Containers such as plastic boxes, jars, and bins to hold small hardware.
- Cleaning supplies in a portable basket or caddy. Make up multiple sets of basic cleaning supplies, and put them in several places to save you running from one room to another or one floor to another at cleaning time. You'll be a lot more inclined to scrub out your bathroom sink or wipe the bathroom mirror if you've got cleaning powder or a spray bottle of window cleaner handy under the sink. Think about investing in another vacuum cleaner for the upstairs if you hate to lug the one you have up and down. You just might find yourself cleaning a bit more often and keeping up on the dirt by having supplies at the ready. Besides, you'll save yourself oodles of time on cleaning day.

YOU'LL THANK YOURSELF LATER

Maximize your utility areas—it will make everything else run smoother if you get these areas systematized!

Getting Time on Your Side

	The Old Way	The Lazy Way
Filing today's mail	30 minutes	30 seconds
Finding today's mail	1 hour	30 seconds
Time spent waiting at the bank	18 minutes (a Friday at 5:15 p.m.)	3 minutes (Tuesday at 9:30 a.m.)
Gathering the supplies to gift-wrap a present	14 minutes	1 minute
Looking up your brother-in-law's work address	23 minutes and 2 telephone conversations	45 seconds in your updated address book
Finding an envelope in which to mail a book	35 minutes	2 minutes

Bringing In the Heavy Hitters

Here are the heavy hitters: The big or bulky or expensive or high-tech items that you might or—get this— might not need to manage your time effectively.

An essential piece to put in place for good time-management results is a work space; whether it's a corporate office or a nook in the kitchen, you just gotta have it. This area is the most important spot in your work life, where you take care of business and do your paperwork. Your work area—let's call it the office, for simplicity's sake—should be appropriately equipped for the jobs you perform with the highest quality products and tools you can afford.

AIM HIGH

An investment in the right equipment will pay big dividends. For example, a computer system that is fast and that has a big hard drive will be worth the slightly higher price tag than one that you'll have to replace in a year.

Read on and take a look at things you might need in your new, highly efficient life.

COMPUTERS

This book is not the place to advise you on computer systems, but here are some guidelines to keep in mind if you're considering one or shopping for your first or a replacement setup:

- Get help. There's no reason for you to reinvent the wheel and learn everything there is to know about computers before you buy or use one. Hire, beg, or trade with a computer-savvy person who will walk through the decision-making process with you. He or she will need to know exactly what your computer needs are, what you do on the computer now, and what kind of functions you're likely to end up doing in the future.

- Remember, buy more hard drive than you think you'll need. It's amazing how the smaller the "boxes" become and the more capacity they hold, the faster we fill them up with information.

- If you're new to computers, you'll have to make the decision between a PC (which is an IBM or similarly operated computer) or a Macintosh. Hands down, the Mac is the easiest and most fun to learn. The PCs, however, offer more software choices because there are more of them. If you're going to be doing any desktop publishing or graphic work, get a Mac. If you're connected in any way to a group already working with PCs, go with an IBM clone.

YOU'LL THANK YOURSELF LATER

All the equipment in the world isn't going to do you much good if you don't know how to use it properly. Hire help—a tutor or consultant—to get you started or to learn about the advanced features of your computer or other machines.

Get a modem. Once a fancy add-on, a modem is almost essential these days. This device connects your computer to a telephone line, enabling you to get on the Web, send and receive email, and transfer information back and forth by fax. Because all documents are on your computer hard drive, you have less paper to worry about—unless you print a hard copy of something.

Dialing Direct

Modems can come as part of your computer (an "internal" modem) or be added as a separate piece of equipment. Speed is of the essence; trust me when I advise you to get as fast a modem as you can afford.

Here's why you don't want to be without a modem:

The first advantage of a modem is its fax feature. If you've got a standalone fax machine, you have to write a memo on your computer, wait for it to print, walk over to the fax machine, punch buttons, and watch while it connects and slowly transmits. With a fax modem, you'll write your memo and press a button to fax it directly from the computer. You'll never see a piece of paper during the transaction. I discuss the advantages of using a fax later in this chapter; the same advantages will apply to the fax connected to your computer modem.

The second thing a modem will do for you is enable you to send and receive email. This can be a blessing or a curse: Email speeds communications by sending

A COMPLETE WASTE OF TIME

The 3 Worst Things to Do when Getting a Computer:

1. Fail to ask for advice from a professional.

2. Assume that if it costs more, it's better.

3. Ignore your personal needs (or let someone else tell you what you need your computer to do for you).

I personally couldn't live now without email, having used it for only a year. I can type a few lines and send it off to clients, children, or friends and feel like I'm doing a better job at keeping in touch. I say more about email later.

information with the push of a button. On the other hand, it's another way for people to access you—in addition to the telephone, letters, pagers, and faxes—so having to check your email creates another chore on your to-do list every day or so.

- Modems let you access the World Wide Web (or Internet) through online services such as America Online or CompuServe. The quantity of information you can retrieve on the Web is beyond belief, and if you're not careful, it will overwhelm you. However, if you use it properly—with moderation and focus— the Web can be an important tool in helping you to use your time effectively and adding to your knowledge base.

Ready, Set, Scan!

Also an integral part of a complete computer system, a scanner can be a helpful tool. Dropping in price even as you read this, scanners are becoming one of the most affordable "accessories" your computer can have. They work by "reading" images and text directly into your computer, where they can be resized, colored, stretched, manipulated, and then printed or emailed. The most common kind looks like a small copier with a glass window on which you lay your picture or printed text.

Be warned, however: Your scanner won't work without the appropriate software installed in your computer. Don't worry; several kinds of software let you further manipulate your scanned images.

Scanned images will take up a lot of space on your hard drive, so you need to consider the size of your computer's hard drive if you want a scanner. Speak with a computer expert if you're unsure about which scanner will be best for both you and your computer.

THE TELEPHONE

Although a discussion of specific telephone equipment is not appropriate here, I do have some telephone-related suggestions you should keep in mind:

- Allow yourself enough telephone lines. At the very least, in a home office situation, you need two lines: one line for the telephone and one to share between the fax modem—whether it's a standalone or your computer's internal one—and your online needs. (These two lines are in addition to your personal or family telephone line).

- If you spend a lot of time on the telephone, don't for a moment forget the impact of a telephone headset. Lightweight and easy to use, a headset keeps your arms free, your neck flexible, and your shoulders relaxed. You can get headsets to fit any kind of phone and phone system. They're also available as remote sets, so you can wander around while you talk.

- If there is any gridlock at the telephones in your house, seriously consider adding another line. I won't get into the subject of coping with chatty teenagers, but carefully weigh the time you might

QUICK ⬤ PAINLESS

More ways to learn about new software, advanced techniques for using your software, or the Internet include instructional videos and CDs provided by manufacturers. Check whether the companies that made your equipment or programs offer these learning tools.

save if you often find yourself waiting to use the phone.

- The cellular phone is another good-news/bad-news invention. Yes, if you run out of gas on the freeway at 11 PM some night, you will thank your lucky stars that you can call for help without having to take a long walk in the dark. The flip side is that you can't hide out successfully if you own a cell phone. Being able to track you down while you're in a meeting or in the bread aisle of the grocery store might be great for your clients and friends but lousy for your concentration and focus.

THE MAGIC OF REPRODUCTION

You could take almost anything away from me except my copier. If you're working by yourself, in a home office or running a household, I think one of the best investments you can make is a copy machine. Just imagine the number of trips you make to the copy center, the number of times projects get put on hold, and the correspondence that can't be sent or files closed because "I just need to make a quick copy of this." If you haven't got a copier close by, "quick" is not how your copies will happen.

Of course, the spectrum of copiers available, each with vastly different arrays of bells and whistles, is enormous. (Why do we get so many choices of virtually any product we buy, from oatmeal to copiers?) In my small home office, I use a Canon Personal Copier, which has served me trouble-free for years.

QUICK ⬤ PAINLESS

Don't give out your cell phone number unless it's absolutely essential. You might share it with your top client and your children—period. You'll save yourself a lot of time and money this way. Better yet—just turn off your cell phone when you don't want to (or shouldn't) be disturbed.

I advise you to overbuy a bit, ending up with a slightly more feature-rich and higher volume copier than you need right now. If you're in business, this strategy will allow for growth and success!

ELECTRONIC ORGANIZERS AND THEIR ALIASES

Also known as PIMs (Personal Information Managers) and PDAs (Personal Data Assistants), electronic organizers are the latest in tiny technology. The information here might be outdated as soon as I type these words. But, no matter—you'll recognize the latest generation of PIMs on the market no matter when you read this.

PIMs are small, hand-held whiz kids that can help anyone who can't sit at her desk all day and who needs to keep a lot of information handy. About the size of a shirt pocket, these organizers are relatively lightweight and can go anywhere with you. You can find electronic organizers that can do the following:

- Keep your address book.
- Hold your to-do list.
- Provide a note pad on which to write.
- Allow you to play games.
- Keep your expense reports current.
- Store a calendar for scheduling on the run.
- Receive email.
- Prompt you with an audible alarm.

IF YOU'RE SO
INCLINED

If you can afford it, purchase a copier with shrink and enlarge capabilities. You can't imagine how often you will need to transform a legal-size sheet of paper into letter size or blow up that tiny newspaper clipping so that it's readable.

Some PIMs can work in tandem with your desk computer so that information can be transferred from one to the other—with the help of a cable between the two—keeping them both current.

3Com's Palm III, the evolved Palm Pilot organizer that is popular, has infrared transfer capabilities, so you and another Palm III user can trade information by just beaming your machines at each other.

Another feature offered by the Palm III is, with the help of an add-on modem, the ability to connect with your desktop computer. You can also write on the Palm III with a stylus; your letters instantly are "read" and transformed into "type."

You'll hear me harp on this more than once in this book, and here it comes again: You've got to have an office to manage your paper—and thus your time—speedily. Chapter 9 is going to walk you through the fine details of setting up an office. Before you can do the finishing touches, however, you want the basics in place. Here are some issues to think about when establishing a new work area or modifying an inefficient one.

Your work surface is crucial, and here's one area where you want as much as you can get. Desks come in virtually hundreds of configurations, from an old door plopped down on two file cabinets to teak executive suites. What's most important is how your desk works for you. Multiple work surfaces—at least two—placed at angles to each other work best:

■ A galley arrangement with two perpendicularly arranged surfaces is a good one; you, on your wheeled chair, can simply twist around to access more work room.

■ If you have a work surface between the two perpendicular ones, you end up with an U-shaped area. You can find desks and modular units designed to incorporate corners.

■ An L-shaped arrangement is the third most common option. Most office furniture manufacturers offer desks with a complementary "return"—the short side of the L. Returns are often lower in height than the desk and were originally used to hold a typewriter. These days, a return in the same height as the desk might be more useful to you; computer monitors can sit at desk height and the keyboard can rest on a keyboard tray just under the desk's top. Depending upon the layout of your office, you can place your return on the left or right side of your desk.

Each one of these arrangements assumes that you have a primary work area—most often close to the computer and telephone. The secondary area might be where you keep tools and supplies you use a lot—perhaps your open planner, stapler, tape, and clock.

Another important requirement is easily accessed storage space within reach of your chair. Most often, this space is file drawers built into a desk plus smaller drawers for supplies. It can also mean being close to a shelf or bookcase.

YOU'LL THANK YOURSELF LATER

When arranging an office, keep lighting issues in mind. Facing a window might be too bright; the window behind you might cause glare on your computer monitor screen.

With these principles in mind, take an objective look at your office. (Better yet, bring in a friend or colleague; fresh eyes often yield fresh ideas.) Is your office organized to maximize your productivity? Here are some questions to ask yourself:

- Is the telephone where you need it to be?
- Do you have to lean over something to use the adding machine—10 times a day?
- Are your computer floppies close to your computer?
- Are there dark spots in your work area that the lamps don't impact?
- Do you fight glare from windows or other light sources on your computer screen?
- Are your only files across the room?
- Do you have any pieces of unused furniture taking up space?
- Are you too close to a noisy wall, always cold because you're near a drafty window, or too accessible to other people because you're close to the door?
- Is there room to meet with others comfortably? Is there room to meet with others—but you never see people in your office?
- When was the last time you shuffled furniture around and tried another layout?

Experiment and get your working environment as streamlined and comfortable as you possibly can. It will pay off in productivity and efficiency.

IF YOU'RE SO
INCLINED

If you need many small supplies close at hand, try a compact storage unit with shelves or drawers (or a combination of both) on wheels. You can pull this unit close when you need it and wheel it out of the way when you don't. Artists' supply stores often sell these.

ERGONOMICS

A smooth functioning office will display more than just a pretty face. Another important consideration is ergonomics—the science of adapting our environment to our bodies (rather than the other way around). This means, in the context of our office discussion, picking equipment and furniture designed to respond well to natural movements, support any weak areas, and prevent stressful motion.

The bonus to ergonomically designed workspaces is more efficient work practices. Ignoring ergonomics often means pain, soreness, fatigue, and eventually repetitive motion injuries such as Carpal Tunnel Syndrome and tendonitis. Following are some items for you to consider. Look in the resource chapter (Appendix C, "Where To Find It") for sources for these products.

Sitting Down on the Job

Your chair is a key purchase and should be as comfortable as possible—without being a lounger. Good back support is essential, and chair height must be adjustable. Top-of-the-line models offer adjustable backrests and headrests, armrest height and width adjustments, and forward and backward seat tilt adjustments.

Many chairs have inflatable back support features that match the natural curve of your back. You should make sure that your thighs are parallel to the floor when seated in your chair with your feet flat on the floor.

IF YOU'RE SO
INCLINED

Using a corner of the room can significantly increase the space in your office. Tuck your desk or its return into the corner, and watch your floor space expand.

Typing Away

Keyboards can be instruments of torture over time and can inflict significant damage if you do a lot of typing. Be sure to invest in a keyboard that feels right, fits your hand and fingers, tilts to a comfortable angle, and rests at the right height.

Putting Your Feet Up

Not only do feet benefit from a footrest, but ankles and legs do, too. Slightly elevating the feet can relieve stress on the legs and reduce back pain and fatigue.

Can We Get a Little Help Back Here?

Your back needs support, initially from your chair. If you need to pad a chair to fit you better, or fill in some gaps between you and the back of your chair, there are an array of cushions, pads and pillows to keep you aligned and comfortable.

Watching Your Work

Place your computer screen so that the top of the screen is about eye level when you're looking straight ahead. Use a monitor arm to get yours in the correct position. You can also use a monitor stand, which holds paper handy to the monitor. Cut down on glare, which can irritate eyes and cause fatigue, with an anti-glare screen.

Helpful Rodents?

You should choose a mouse and mouse pad with your hands and wrists in mind—not the cute picture or the color. Wrists are particularly prone to repetitive

YOU'LL THANK YOURSELF LATER

Carting your laptop around can play havoc with your body. Choose a carrying case carefully; load it with what you will be transporting and check for balance and ease. Be sure it has a shoulder strap or can be carried on your back, backpack-style.

movement injury, so protect them with cushions, foam pads, and the right keyboard platform. Pads are made for keyboards, mouse pads, and even adding machines. You can also wear lightweight wrist supports to keep your wrists in the proper position.

Standing Up to the Task

Another computer accessory for heavy typing is a copy holder. Also called a document holder, it attaches to your monitor or sits on your desktop to hold your copy at a comfortable height and angle. This handy tool is inexpensive, takes up hardly any room, and can reduce eye, back, and neck strain.

Up or Down?

Adjustable-height work surfaces can significantly reduce fatigue and muscle strain. Altering the position of your hands, wrists, feet, and legs is crucial to preventing tension. Many people have found that moving the whole body from a sitting to a standing position keeps them working longer and feeling better. Several companies make adjustable workstations that are easily raised and lowered.

Bits and Pieces

Some smaller items have been adapted to meet ergonomic concerns: Pens with soft, contoured rubber grips reduce muscle strain and stress. A "gliding" stapler remover is much easier on the hands and fingers than the conventional claw type. An electric envelope opener saves wear on the hands and fingers. Several types of

QUICK ⬤ PAINLESS

Three ergonomic tips: Keep your wrist in a neutral position when using the mouse. Your mouse and keyboard should be at the same level. Don't rest your palm or wrists on the wrist pad.

Like a new pair of shoes, it's hard to know how equipment is going to feel until you've used it for awhile. Ask the sales person whether you can try new equipment or furniture for a week before committing to the purchase.

gloves minimize vibration and support the wrists when you use power tools.

Any ergonomic expert will advise you to keep moving. Take breaks from your typing, and exercise your hands. There are soft rubber "toys" made for squeezing and strengthening your grip and increasing hand motion. Get up frequently and walk around. If you're not using a headset, move the phone receiver from one ear to the other every few minutes. Raise or lower your footrest so your feet change height a few times a day.

Getting Time on Your Side

	The Old Way	The Lazy Way
How late, on average, your expense report is every month	2 weeks	It's not!
Sending a fax	4.5 minutes	4.5 seconds
Making a copy of your insurance card	30 minutes (to drive to the copy center)	2 minutes (including the warm-up time of your own copier)
Looking up information about when to plant bulbs in your garden	3 hours at the library	48 minutes on the Web
Copying a recipe to send to Aunt Kay	1 hour (including the drive to a copy center)	23 minutes (scanned, printed, and in the mail)
How often you connect with your cousin Kim	Once a year, on her birthday (if you remember!)	Once a month by email

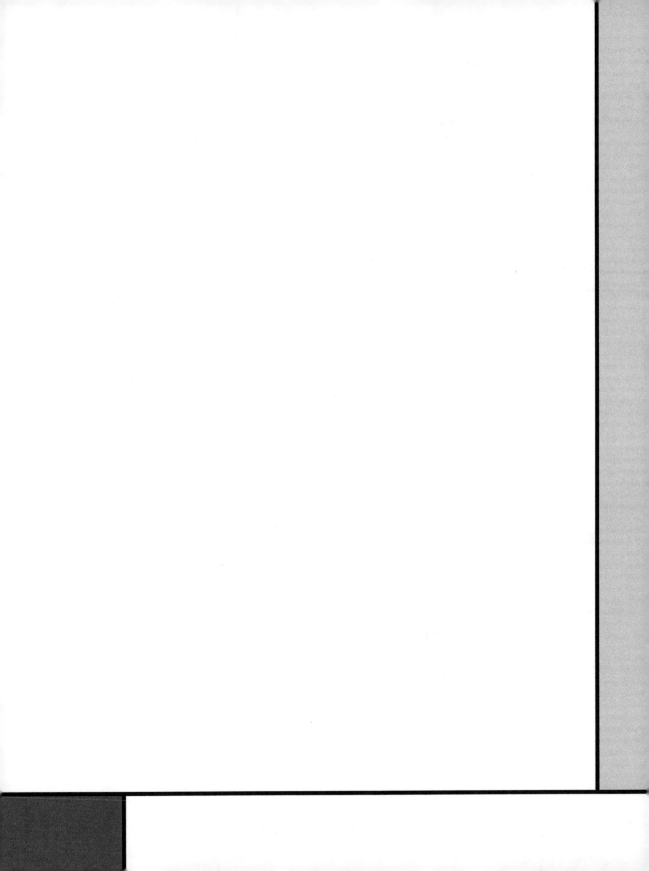

Part 2

Planning Before, After, and Through

Are You Too Lazy to Read "Planning Before, After, and Through"?

1 Do the only baskets in your house appear just at Easter? ☐ yes ☐ no

2 Your paperwork is grouped together—in grocery bags. ☐ yes ☐ no

3 Your planner is where your kids find a blank piece of paper to draw on. ☐ yes ☐ no

Getting the Ball Rolling

Managing your time well involves *investing* your time well—putting time into activities that will pay off in the future. Just as saving your money now will reward you in the future, making a little extra effort now will save time down the line.

You probably have done many of the following "investment" activities, but here's a list to jog your memory. I hope you can get inspired to take the time now and ease the way for future time savings. I explain in more detail some of the items I list:

- Program your telephone's speed-dial numbers.

- Set up voice-mail groups so you can send the same message to a specific group. For example, a group could include all your employees or just your sales people.

- Enter your fax's programmed numbers.

- Set up your fax to take advantage of its broadcast fax feature.

- Before a vacation, prepare labels for postcards you'll send while you're away. (And don't forget to pack the labels!)

- Print stationery with all your information on it.

- Print up business cards—even if you're not in business.

- Print shipping labels with your return address.

- Pre-address several envelopes to people or companies to whom you often send things. For example, if you mail health insurance claim forms once a week or so, make a supply of envelopes so they're ready to go when you are.

- Write a brief synopsis of your medical history.

- Do the same for each family member.

- Design and print forms for things you need to track regularly.

- Make rubber stamps with information you need to write often.

- Get a postage scale and an assortment of stamps; stay away from the post office.

- Do your banking online; stay out of banks.

- Keep your car's gas tank full. (If you have a teenager, that might be the easiest thing on this list!)

- Enter all your names and addresses into the computer or address book.

- Set up a system for gift giving. You'll read more about this later, but basically, a gift-giving system means having everything you need—from the actual gifts to a small supply of wrapping supplies and cards—ready to go at a moment's notice. Believe it or not, this simple technique can work wonders.

A COMPLETE WASTE OF TIME

The 3 Worst Things You Can Do when Getting Organized:

1. Put it off.

2. Think you don't need to do it.

3. Fail to bring in a professional.

- Buy presents in advance and when you see them.

- Send in your film for developing. They send new film back with your prints, so you've saved at least two trips to the store.

- Write all recurring important dates in your planner at the beginning of the year.

DIALING DIRECT

Programming your speed-dial numbers will, over the long haul, save you time. I really hope you don't have *all* of these techno toys, but program what you have: your email addresses, cell phone, your computer's fax program, and your personal organizer.

Another way to keep track of numbers is to make lists and post them by the equipment you'll be using:

- Cell phone numbers on a sheet in the car. (Put it in a plastic sheet protector.)

- A list of the fax numbers you have to dial manually.

- A list of frequently called numbers from home: the video store, the pizza parlor, and the veterinarian.

FINDING THAT SPECIAL SOMETHING

Present shopping—if you're like me, you put off buying presents until the last moment. Getting to a store and picking out just the right thing seems so daunting—especially when you're short on time and low on inspiration. So you put it off until you're walking out the door to the birthday party in a panic or shipping something

QUICK ⬤ *PAINLESS*

Get into the habit of using the telephone to order presents. Most local stores can handle your telephoned order, gift-wrap it, and either ship it or have it ready for you to pick up.

(expensively) overnight to get it to the recipient on time.
Silly.

Try this system: Have a few tried 'n true standby presents (or ideas for presents) always on hand. Here are
some suggestions that I think you'll find virtually always
appreciated and that show your thoughtfulness. Note
that most of these presents get used and used up. Avoid
buying more stuff for people who already own too much
stuff. You won't be doing your friends or relatives—or
the environment—any favors. Here are some gift ideas
that won't end up as land fill):

- **Gift certificates.** Book stores and department stores
  for adults, music stores and clothing shops for teens,
  and a toy store for kids. Many of these can be handled with a phone call or ordered online.

- **Something green.** Plants or cut flowers from the
  local nursery, ordered online or from your florist.

- **Movies.** Passes or gift certificates for local theaters.

- **Charity.** A donation in the recipient's name.

- **Subscriptions.** Magazines or foreign newspapers for
  readers.

- **Beauty and health.** Spa treatments, facials, massages, manicures and pedicures, and exotic herbal or
  mud treatments.

- **Services.** A day's visit from a cleaning service, a couple of hours with a computer tutor, an astrology
  reading, or a wardrobe consultation. If you really
  want to make an impression, give a gift certificate
  from a professional organizer.

- ■ **Music.** Tapes or CDs.

- ■ **Inspiration.** Books on tape, from adventure to spiritual. Tickets to a lecture series or the cost of a retreat are other ideas to try.

- ■ **Food.** A wonderful cake from your favorite bakery or the best smoked salmon you can find.

Another do-ahead technique is to keep a small supply of presents on hand, stashed for last-minute gift-giving. An inspiring book, attractive note cards, candles, or a good bottle of wine can be among your present inventory.

Don't forget greeting cards: Collect a varied assortment that you can pull out at a moment's notice and send off or tuck into a present.

The last gift-giving element is wrapping. *The Lazy Way* is, of course, to have your gift wrapped at the store, but if that's not possible, you need the right stuff at home to do the job.

I suggest just two wrapping papers and two to three types of ribbon. If you choose the right colors and basic patterns, these supplies will meet every gift-wrapping need that comes your way. Plain glossy paper in a solid color is one good choice, as is a second paper in a non-holiday, abstract pattern. Choose ribbons or bows to match both papers and you will be able to produce smashing-looking birthday, anniversary, baby shower, Mother's and Father's day, and Easter gifts, all from the same supplies! (Get your gift-wrapping inventory in bulk, on rolls, from a discount paper store.)

QUICK ●n● PAINLESS

I use white paper and change the ribbon to fit the occasion: red ribbon for Christmas or Valentine's, pale blue or pink for babies, and gold or silver for wedding gifts and friends.

BEING BUSINESS-LIKE

I'm pretty adamant on the subject of letterhead and business cards for everyone. Obviously, if you're in business, you already have these tools. This is directed to those of you without a corporate identity who often still need to give out your name, address, telephone and fax numbers, and sometimes a cell phone number and email address. Why dictate this information continually? Print some simple cards (you can be creative and make them great-looking while you're at it) and carry them with you.

I promise you, you'll end up using your cards at the repair shop, the department store, the vet's, and the coffee shop for the nice couple you just met. Once you see that you're spending less time repeating yourself when you have some business cards in your arsenal, you'll wonder why you never thought of it before. Plus, it will cut down on the frequency of people losing your number or never getting in touch with you because they couldn't read their own handwriting.

KEEPING TRACK OF ALL THOSE NUMBERS AND DATES

Your address book, in whatever form you prefer—a paper book with listings written by hand, paper that is computer-generated, or totally electronic—can be a boon in your time-saving efforts. Use your address book for more than names and addresses. Here's what else you can track:

IF YOU'RE SO
INCLINED

Remember, you don't have to be in business to use your own card. Go to your local printers and have them help you design a snappy-looking business card. Pick out good paper, a legible font, and colorful ink and let your imagination loose. (A tip for baby boomers: Keep the typeface fairly large.)

- Social Security numbers of all your family members (under "S").

- Your recurring prescription numbers next to the pharmacy phone number.

- Birthdays (if you don't already have them written in your planner).

- Your vehicles' policy numbers with your auto insurance company.

- Your health insurance policy number with your insurance customer service number.

- Frequent flyer account numbers with your travel agent's listing.

FORMS ARE US!

Making forms to track things can be a big help if you have a lot of information you must keep updated. Use a ledger pad or make a form on the computer to breeze through record-keeping. When I first started my business, I made a form for tracking billable hours. At the end of every month, I had a record of the hours I'd spent with each client, making invoicing a less arduous (and much speedier) task than it would have been without the form.

Financial Forms

To this day, I still use a form I devised to keep track of donated gift certificates I contribute to fund-raising events. Every time I send a donation, I note the date and name of the event, the organization holding it, and the expiration date of my certificate.

IF YOU'RE SO
INCLINED

A computer is worth its weight in gold if for no other reason than to keep order among the names, addresses, and many numbers everyone seems to have. My impression is that everyone is changing area codes or adding email addresses almost daily, and the computer makes these changes and additions a snap.

Forming Up for Chores

Tracking kids' jobs and chores is another candidate for a homemade form. You only have to make it once and then copy it over and over. A form to gather information from new or potential clients relieves you of having to remember which questions to ask.

Medicine by the List

I made a form for elderly clients who have a lot of drugs to take several times a day. The chart shows when each medication should be taken. Whoever refills their plastic pill holders for the week just has to follow the chart.

Getting Fit with Forms

Get fit by tracking your exercise routine on paper. You can make a chart of the specific exercises you need to perform on particular days. You might even find it handy—and a good reminder—to make a copy of the chart and put it somewhere visible ... perhaps the refrigerator?

GETTING STUFF TO YOU EASILY

This might be scary, but think for a minute about how many times you find yourself sitting down, usually on a gorgeous day, writing and rewriting your return address. More Saturday afternoons have been wasted with this seemingly unimportant task! Well, now's the time to take back those weekends. Here's a few ideas to get you finished with mailings and out with your family faster.

Label-Ease!

Get mailing labels printed to save time. If you have to send large envelopes often, or do a lot of catalog shopping (and returning), self-stick mailing labels will shorten the time it takes to prepare an envelope or package for shipping. (American Stationery Company has nice ones; see Appendix C, "Where to Find It.")

CUTTING DOWN ON REPETITIOUS TASKS

Now that we've tackled the return address situation, let's move on to all those other things that you do over and over again, day after day, week after week. It's simple— with a little do-ahead—to conquer those tasks!

Simply Stamping

You can use rubber stamps for more than return addresses. Get one to endorse your checks quickly; you don't have to run a business to take advantage of business tools. Get stamps with the kids' names on them; use them for school papers, folders, lunch bags, and identifying their books.

Gracefully Grabbing Groceries

You can create your shopping list in advance to avoid writing out the basics over and over again. Here's what to do: Make a list of the things you regularly purchase at the grocery store, and put them in the order they're found in the store.

But hold on! You don't have to write down every spice you might ever need; just make a line for "spices"

QUICK  PAINLESS

Make up a general shopping list, photocopy it, and post one on the fridge. Circle items as you run out and when you're ready to shop, just grab your list and go!

Rubber stamps are the way to go, but stamp pads that dry out are not. Be sure you get rubber stamps that are self-inking.

and you can fill in the specifics as the need occurs. Make several copies of your master list and post it in the kitchen.

As you run low on—or out of—items, everyone in the family should circle or put a check mark next to the item on the list. That way, when you're flying out the door to go to the store, you'll have—in a perfect world—a complete shopping list ready to go.

MEDICALLY SPEAKING

Writing down your medical history can be invaluable every time you fill out a doctor's forms and have to remember ancient history. I've written down my information, and I update it on the rare occasions something changes or if I'm prescribed a new medication to treat an ailment. It's good to know which treatments worked and which did not.

You'll find the same benefit with your children's information, especially if you need the information in a hurry. I faxed my boys' information to the school nurse when necessary, and if they had to see a new doctor, it saved so much time. I only had to gather the information once and update it occasionally. Seeing a doctor can be a stressful situation all on its own, so make it easier on yourself by having your facts and figures at the ready.

CHECKING IT OUT

Another great technique to save you time is to use checklists. A list will save you the effort of reinventing the wheel every time you must do something. Remember, the less you have to think and remember, the easier your life will be. Checklists help you avoid cluttering your brain with all that remembered information.

Here are just a few examples of when checklists will come in handy:

- Packing before trips
- Gathering presentation materials
- Preparing menus
- Setting up for meetings
- Entertaining and parties
- Moving

SET UP SYSTEMS

The more you can make systems of tasks you do over and over again, the less time you will spend doing them. Anything that you can take the time to put together in advance will free you during busy periods. And you'll always have the things or information you need on hand when you need them:

- A huge time-saver is to get your wardrobe organized. Getting dressed is an activity most of us face every single morning, and the more pared down and organized your wardrobe is, the more time you will save.
- You might send potential clients information packets when they call; prepare (or have someone else prepare) a supply of these packages so they're ready to go at a moment's notice. You'll not only save

YOU'LL THANK YOURSELF LATER

Enlist the services of a wardrobe consultant or a professional organizer who specializes in closets and wardrobes. You will save an enormous amount of time whipping your wardrobe into shape, which will, in turn, save you minutes every day (and hours in the long run)!

time, but also your professionalism will be apparent to your prospect.

- New customers often need materials, samples, and forms from you; collect them and prepare them for mailing in advance to the extent you can.

- Fill out a master health insurance claim form with the required information that stays the same for every claim. Make copies and then fill in only the variable information on the form when you file a claim.

Write It Down

Putting routines and information on paper can save you a heck of a lot of verbal explaining. Here are some times when you want everything in writing:

- If you often use temporary office help, they will undoubtedly benefit from a list you've prepared for them in advance. Arming them with your biggest clients' names, addresses, and telephone numbers will save them—and you—a lot of time.

- Documenting your routines is another enormous help when delegating chores. Write down each step of your banking procedure, for example: how to endorse the checks, fill out deposit slips, find the bank-by-mail envelopes, and make notations in your checkbook or computer.

- Make charts of duties and chores; for example, on a grid format, list children and their jobs.

- Write down the evening routine for the babysitter, along with emergency numbers, neighbors' names, and so on.

Double Up

Sometimes, under certain conditions, it makes a lot of sense to multitask—a new word for doing two or more things simultaneously. All of us instinctively tend to combine activities and for good reason: You can leverage your time to accomplish more. Here are some ideas that you might not have thought of and that might inspire you to multitask to the max.

Things to do while driving:

- Listen to audio tapes.
- When necessary, have a conversation on your cell phone. (Use extreme caution if you must do this; pull off the road and stop if you must take notes.)
- Talk to your spouse (but only if he or she is in the car!).
- Practice your speech.
- Listen to your child.
- Think.

Things to do while on the telephone:

- Have a long, catch-up conversation with a friend with a dust rag or sponge in hand. (I often tackle the refrigerator during one of these calls.)
- Stretch, standing up or lying down. (Be careful about heavy breathing, though!)

QUICK ⬤ *PAINLESS*

Save time and hassle in the mornings by being clever the night before: Pack up the car with the shoes to be returned, the tickets to be dropped off, and the kids' backpacks. Everything will be in place before you run out the door.

- Polish the silver.
- Iron.
- File papers.
- Fold laundry.
- Shine shoes.

Things to do while watching TV:

- Iron.
- Knit or do other handiwork.
- Fold clean clothes.
- Do stretching exercises or sit on the exercise bike. (I mean *pedal* on the bike!)
- Give yourself a manicure.
- Braid your little girl's hair.
- Sort your change and roll your coins.

Some other multitasking activities:

- Prepare dinner while coaching your child through his spelling words.
- Read while on the Stairmaster or exercise bike.
- Open your mail or read while waiting at the dentist's office.
- Prune the roses while discussing your child's book report.
- Do needlework while you listen to your child's account of her day.
- Join a car pool or take the bus; use commuting time to gather your thoughts or catch up on reading.
- Write personal notes while on an airplane.

A COMPLETE WASTE OF TIME

The 3 Worst Things to Do while Driving:

1. Dial your cell phone.

2. Read.

3. Balance a cup of hot coffee, a doughnut, and the steering wheel.

Getting Time on Your Side

	The Old Way	The Lazy Way
Number of books you've "read" in the last month	$^1/_2$	3—you've been listening to books on tape while commuting
Number of weeks in a row you've tested your child's spelling words	2 max	Every week, now that you do it while washing the dishes
Time spent telling someone your name, address, and telephone number	3 minutes	No time at all— you hand him your business card
Time spent at the bank per month	55 minutes	0—online banking to the rescue
Time spent finding your frequent flyer account number	12 minutes	30 seconds— it's in your address book
Getting out the door in the morning	7 minutes	30 seconds— everything was done last night

Delegate, Delegate, Delegate...

If I've said it once, I've said it a thousand times: Anything worth doing is worth delegating to someone else. This is especially true if you happen to hate the chore at hand or if you're totally unqualified to do it. Carefully choosing helpers can dramatically increase your productive time by freeing you from routine or time-consuming duties.

THE OL' TIME VERSUS MONEY DILEMMA

The biggest trade-off, most probably, is money: There is always the issue of budgeting to hire help. But sometimes, it simply is essential that you spend some money so that you can better deal with money-making activities, alleviate a bottleneck, avoid a crisis, or simply ease your mind. In other words, money might not buy you everything, but it will buy you time.

Delegating needn't always be costly. I've also got some suggestions for low- and no-cost ways to find help. Consider saving on some big-ticket items so that you can afford the

time to enjoy your life. A big-screen television isn't worth the money if you never have the time to watch it. Stick with the smaller TV and watch more movies with your kids.

MY WAY OR THE FREEWAY?

Another stumbling block to delegating is that we're all creatures of habit and have developed our own ways of doing things. Now of course, it might actually take some self-control for you to give up control, but that's okay! The idea is to find someone good and let him or her deal with the project at hand. Of course, you need to keep an eye on things, especially at the beginning of a delegated project, but you must also let good people do what they do best—even if it isn't the way you would have done it.

Here are the delegating rules and regulations:

- Always explain exactly what you want from your helper.

- Always give a due date.

- When necessary, teach the steps required to perform the task and explain why it has to be done just the way you're teaching.

- Stay out of the way!

HOUSEHOLD HELPERS

If your job is running a home, think like a business. Money might not be the object; the commodity called time might be what's in short supply. You can apply business-like principles to homemaking.

Get Your Priorities Straight

What's more important, a clean refrigerator or two children needing to cuddle with Mom or Dad? If you reason that a business's goal is to make money, the CEO should be making money. If a parent's job is to raise kids, then the parent should be reading stories. Both should, when possible, leave extraneous tasks to others.

WHOM TO DO WHAT AND WHERE?

What to delegate and to whom are the target questions. There are thousands of tasks to be performed in the home every week. Come up with your personal list of the most onerous and see how you can affordably get someone else to do them. Think creatively about the possibilities for getting them done.

Checks and Balances

When it comes to bill paying, consider finding someone to come in twice a month to a stack of bills, write out the checks for your signature, stamp and address the envelopes, file the bills, take the payments to the post office, and wish them goodbye. On the way out the door, she can tell you how much you've got left in your bank balance.

Happy Housekeeping

Housecleaning is self-explanatory, but remember that some housekeepers will do windows, sweep up outside, clean out the garage, and rearrange the children's toys. Think in terms of expanding the definition of "cleaning"

YOU'LL THANK YOURSELF LATER

You don't need to be raking in the big bucks to have a financial assistant—help might be as close as the next room!

to include those projects that have been on your to-do list for more than three years.

Tiptoe Through the Tulips

Some of you undoubtedly like to putter in the garden, so delegate the parts you don't want to do. Gardening help comes in all forms, from mow 'n blow services to landscaping firms to the kid next door looking for a little extra money in exchange for raking the leaves.

Laundry Loader

When it comes to the laundry, delegating in this area might take some training if you have a system you prefer, but why not hire someone twice a week to run the washing machine, tack buttons on clothes, and iron and put away everything clean?

Food Forays

Hiring someone to do your grocery shopping will, I assure you, save you money—or at least pay for itself. Armed with a detailed list of what you want, a shopper can hit the store and never once be tempted to spend your money on impulse items. Your shopper should come back with what you specified—and nothing else. After a few trial runs, he will know that you prefer your tomatoes "Roma" as opposed to rotten and that you like squishy toilet paper instead of military style.

Another option is using a grocery store that delivers or other food-delivery service. Many accept orders that are faxed, phoned, or processed through the Internet. You can at least keep yourself well supplied with the

basics and make only one weekly trip to the grocery store for extras. I list resources for buying groceries on the Internet in Appendix C, "Where To Find It."

If you can find a dairy in your area to deliver milk and other dairy products, your family will always survive—on cold cereal or canned soups, if necessary—if you don't make it to the store. I shopped much less than usual during the period I had a local dairy deliver. Not only did that save me time, but it also saved me money because I stayed away from the grocery store.

Cookin' with Gas

Someone other than you, standing at your stove, cooking your dinner. Doesn't this sound like heaven? Some of you working parents come home to Monster Hour, phones ringing, errands calling, spouses—if you have one—late or out of town; you arrive to hungry, grumpy children all wanting 100 percent of your attention. You want to either feed their bodies as quickly as possible or delay mealtime so that you can sit down with them and feed their souls. Food already prepared means you can concentrate on the latter activity.

Who can help?

- Perhaps the cleaning person is a wonderful cook; she could cook for you on her regularly scheduled day.

- Maybe you can change the cleaner's schedule (from one whole day) so that she comes two afternoons. That way, someone else could handle meals at least twice that week.

You've worked like a dog all day. Everything went wrong. You're frazzled. Take a break from the kitchen and pick up Chinese takeout or order pizza to be delivered. Everyone will be happy.

The Lazy Way

- The teenager next door—would he or she be interested in putting the pasta water on the stove, setting the table, buttering the garlic bread, and getting the salad in order?
- Are Grandma or Grandpa around?

TAX TRICKS

If you prepare your taxes yourself, seriously consider hiring a tax preparer—a certified public accountant, an enrolled agent, or a tax-preparing franchise such as H&R Block. They have the expertise and the software to prepare your taxes quickly and accurately and in the most advantageous way for you.

If you already have a professional tax-preparer but spend months fretting while you gather your financial bits 'n pieces—scraps of paper, every bill you paid during the last year, every pharmacy receipt, bank-statement inserts, and miscellaneous envelopes—you'd be well advised to hire help. It will save you hours—of both time and mental anguish—if you can find someone skilled in collecting and organizing the information your tax-preparer needs.

Separating the Wheat from the Chaff

Your tax assistant will cull from your files—or those boxes—just the information needed to fill out the "organizer" that your tax-preparer sends to you. She will also supply the preparer with only the necessary documents instead of a year's worth of your personal paper inventory.

A COMPLETE WASTE OF TIME

The 3 Worst Ways to Handle Your Taxes:

1. Not at all.

2. By yourself.

3. Without staying in the know about the latest tax laws.

He or she will also know to collect cash receipts for deductible expenses and which paper can be thrown out. (I'm always amazed at how many people save their grocery receipts and have absolutely no reason for doing so!) This will save your tax preparer and staff several hours of sorting through your information. How does that help you? By only bringing what your preparer needs, you can significantly lower your tax-preparation bill, offsetting the cost of hiring your "tax assistant," whose hourly rates are much less than a CPA's.

Look for a professional organizer or ask your tax-preparer to recommend someone you could hire. Don't forget to inquire of family and friends whether they know anyone who could do the job.

SNAPSHOTS IN A SNAP

The jobs of sorting photographs and making albums are definite contenders for delegation. You can use a young person to stick photos into plastic sleeves or hire a clever friend or professional organizer to put together beautiful albums for you.

Another place I'd look for a photo-album helper is a local representative of "Creative Memories," a company that sells archival grade albums, paper, and the decorating supplies you need to assemble heirloom-quality photo albums. Your local rep or one of his or her customers might well be interested enough to take on your albums.

QUICK ⬤ PAINLESS

A good rule of thumb about which receipts to keep: If you're audited, you most likely will need to show documentation for any expenses you've claimed as a deduction. That means receipts from the video store, pet store, sports shop, and clothing boutique are material for the wastebasket.

MOVIN' AND GROOVIN'

I don't know why, but moving always seems to occur just as you're finishing your thesis or having a baby or starting a business. In other words, it happens at the absolutely wrong time. Even if there's no huge time conflict, moving is a pain. Think about hiring a moving coordinator to make your life a zillion times easier.

A moving coordinator will attend to hundreds of details, such as getting bids on moving companies, overseeing the packing, sending change-of-address forms, and being sure there are toilet paper, light bulbs, and working electricity and telephones at your new home.

If you have elderly parents who need to move, hiring someone to help could be a great investment. Your parents might be hundreds of miles away or physically fragile and might even need help downsizing the amount of belongings they own. Sometimes, an impartial third party can do a better job than stressed-out family members. Besides, you might not be in a position to take time away from work and lose income.

Look for a moving coordinator through moving companies, the phone book, or professional organizers.

MAKE A DATE FOR YOUR ESTATE

An estate organizer might be a relatively new concept, but he is someone who can help you set up an estate plan or implement one after death. Although estate organizers are not qualified to give legal or financial advice, they handle the following tasks:

YOU'LL THANK YOURSELF LATER

A good moving coordinator will encourage you to purge your belongings well before packing begins to reduce the amount to pack and move. This suggestion, by itself, is a money saver. Although you'll have to invest some time at the front end, you'll have a lot less to unpack and deal with at your destination.

- Inventory all your assets with names, numbers, and amounts.

- Make a list of your important contact people and advisors (for example, your bankers, attorney, stockbroker, and so on).

- Organize your insurance documents.

- Ensure that your will is prepared and its location is documented.

- Arrange or provide anything that someone might need to know in case of your disability or death.

An estate organizer should prepare a binder or folder for you with all the pertinent information (which will need to be updated occasionally). It's also the organizer's job to help you review a list of important documents to be sure you have everything you need.

After death, the organizer sees to it that the estate plan is implemented. This can mean working with family members to locate documents, file insurance claims, see that attorneys, banks, accountants, and stockbrokers have the right information and necessary forms, and generally take care of the details at a confusing and stressful time.

Look for an estate organizer among professional organizers, or ask your tax preparer, attorney, or stockbroker for referrals.

IF YOU'RE SO
INCLINED

One of the kindest things you can do is leave your financial information in good order for your heirs. It does mean an investment of time on your part, but you will save your loved ones a lot of time—and a lot of money—if you make that commitment.

Whew! You did it: You got your life organized in a binder. If anything should happen to you, your heirs will now know what to do. Spend some of their inheritance and go away for a long weekend.

The Lazy Way

NAVIGATING INSURANCE ISSUES

I hope you never need one, but in case of a major property loss, consider hiring a private insurance adjuster to handle your claim, watchdog the insurance company, and get the largest settlement possible. Inquire with the National Association of Public Insurance Adjusters in Herndon, VA, and be sure to check references of anyone you're considering.

MEDICAL MADNESS

Another person I hope you never need is a medical claims assistant. However, should you or a loved face chronic or catastrophic illness, rejected medical claims, or confusing claim procedures, you might want to call in a pro. A medical claims professional will act as your advocate, untangle any knotty problems you run into, and get your medical bills covered as fully as possible by your insurance company.

Call the Alliance of Claims Assistance Professionals for tips. Insurance salespeople might also share recommendations. Try the billing person in your doctor's office; he might know of someone savvy in these matters.

DELEGATING AT THE OFFICE

Whatever your work environment, delegating is the key to your success and good use of your time. No one can do it all, nor do it all well. Building relationships with those who can help you will support your efforts in accomplishing more—or working less.

Larger offices might have a pool of assistants—what we used to call secretaries—to help with the myriad tasks that arise every day in a work situation. Although most large chores may have already been delegated, that should not prevent you from hiring a part-time helper to assist you with special projects or routine chores. Even if you have a full-time assistant, there might be situations when adding a short-termer to the mix could get you both through a time crunch.

Before you go full steam ahead into a project all by your lonesome, take a second to think about how you could get other people involved. It will increase your productivity, make those stiff deadlines easier to meet, and generally help everyone. Believe me, those few moments of pre-project delegation deliberation are well worth it.

Other Functions to Farm Out

If you're running a small firm, you have undoubtedly already farmed out some chores. Keep your eyes open to cost- and time-efficient methods to add to the list.

Some areas to think about:

- Human resources
- Bookkeeping
- Accounting
- Meeting planning
- Research for reports
- Payroll
- Accounts receivable

QUICK 🔲 *PAINLESS*

Teach your helpers the fine art of multitasking—for a little extra pay. The babysitter can inspire and teach your kids to bake the brownies needed at school tomorrow. The gardener might be happy to haul off your extra garbage to the dump.

The 3 Worst Things to Do
When Delegating Jobs:

1. Fail to give adequate training. Be clear and specific about what you want done and how to do it, and you'll maximize an employee's productivity. Take the time to train, and you'll reap the benefits.

2. Fail to give them some authority. Let them choose which kind of file folders to buy or have a say in how your database should be set up.

3. Forget to praise them for a job well done. No one gets enough positive feedback and everyone needs it, so do your part!

- Collections
- Travel arrangements
- Purchasing

Self employed? You've got everything on your list—from dusting off the computer screen to doing long-term strategizing to buying pencil lead. Here's where hiring someone to take over some of the routine chores or help you accomplish short-term projects will boost your bottom line or simply keep you sane.

CONQUERING THE COMPUTER

When it comes to a computer, whether you're at home or the office, the fastest way to shorten the learning curve is to hire a tutor. Yes, it costs, but it also costs you money to spend hours and hours flipping through the instruction manuals or waiting on hold for tech support.

The fastest way to proficiency is with a professional. A consultant can help you at any level: from taking the machine out of the box and setting it up for you, to teaching you the basics of a word processing or financial software program, or even walking you through advanced techniques in desktop publishing software. Believe it or not, many of these computer-savvy folks will actually come to your home or office to do the job. Talk about a house call!

More Good News

A great time to enlist a consultant is before you buy something. Whether you're looking at a new computer system or just a new word processing program, it pays to enlist someone who's on your side. Make sure that what you're investing in will answer your specific needs.

Your average salesperson might try to sell the most expensive equipment with all the bells and whistles, but if all you need is a computer to type reports, why let him bully you into a system designed for a computer graphics artist? Make sure that you're buying what you really need.

The same rule goes for purchasing new programs for you to work with, so talk to someone in the know before you buy. If you want a program to make charts for your household, find out the minimum you need to add to your existing system to accomplish that. More importantly, find out if the programs you already have can do it for you. The packages that computer software companies put together are more complete than you might imagine.

Don't let those fat manuals spook you either. You really don't have to learn everything about a new software program that the manual would teach you; your consultant can help you learn only the features you actually use and show you some time-saving shortcuts to boot!

Make some quick calls to the people you know who either use the same software or hardware or are in the same business as you. They should be able to recommend someone to help. But make sure that you are specific about your needs; if you need to know how to set up a spreadsheet for the first time, you might hire a different person from the one who can show you how to make a spreadsheet do complicated calculations.

IF YOU'RE SO INCLINED

Think trade, as in trading services. Your computer guy might want your widgets instead of cash. The payroll company might need your printing services for its next brochure. Just be sure to spell out clearly in advance what your arrangement is and exactly what's being traded.

RIDDING YOURSELF OF THE ROUTINE

Routine chores are the biggest offenders when it comes to keeping stuff on track, so here are more "small" tasks you might be able to delegate:

- Got towering stacks of paper because you haven't filed anything in months? Get someone to put those papers in files so that you can find them again.

- Find a person to do the billing: collecting time sheets, entering figures into the computer, or finding scattered sticky notes all over your desk and consolidating them into a bill—so you can get paid!

- If you ask for it, your assistant will see that things arrive at your desk with the junk mail tossed, reading materials to one side, top priority items on top, and less important communiques lower in the pile. This job alone might save you 45 minutes a day. Say you collect mail 300 times a year; you do the math!

- Deliveries and errands might only take a "few minutes," but each of those minutes adds up. Get someone to do the running around for you.

- Seasonal projects such as a big mailing might involve copying, folding, stuffing envelopes, sealing envelopes, making address labels, sticking labels to envelopes, and getting mail to the post office. You don't have the time.

- Delegate the telephoning. How much time would it save you if you asked another person once a week or every morning to set up or confirm appointments? Try it.

IF YOU'RE SO
INCLINED

Tip the babysitter who did something extra. Write a small article for the company newsletter about the project your assistant successfully completed. Sincerely express your appreciation to the consultant who solved a problem. Reward your team members and keep them motivated.

Getting Time on Your Side

	The Old Way	The Lazy Way
Getting out payroll	6 hours by yourself	20 minutes delegated to a payroll service
Learning your new word-processing program	3 months (by trial and error)	1 month (with the help of a consultant)
Time spent bringing treats to every soccer game during the season	1.5 hours per week	10 minutes per week instructing your helper
Opening and sorting the mail	8 hours every month	Zip
Emptying the waste-baskets	13 minutes every week	Zip
Putting your photographs in albums	Never happened	15 minutes per week, guiding someone you hired to do the job for you

Follow Up and Follow Through

After you've instituted some time-management basics from the following chapters, some special projects, solutions, and ideas I offer in this chapter will serve as your continuing time-management education. Remember this: A well-balanced life means you have time to do *many* things that are important and enjoyable to you. Here are some ideas to help you achieve that balance. Because we all get a bit crazy sometimes, try some of my stress-reduction techniques on the really bad days!

ADVANCE MEDICINE

It is becoming more apparent that we, as consumers, have to begin taking more responsibility for our own medical care. Nothing will get you feeling better faster than being—to the extent that you can—a proactive patient. Waiting to be told what to do and assuming that people are doing what they're supposed to do can be hazardous to your health! You can do

some things that not only will keep everyone on their toes, but also will save you time.

When I had elective surgery a couple of years ago, I saved myself and my doctors' offices a lot of time by using the fax machine. I had to change my primary care physician, stash some blood in advance, visit specialists, and so on. All this medical activity occurred almost two hours away from home. Here's what I did to keep things running smoothly:

■ Before I ever spoke to any medical office, I faxed all the information and records that the doctors needed or that I had. This way, when I called to set up an appointment, the office usually knew who I was and what I needed. My faxes were often already filed with my chart.

■ If the doctor's office needed me to fill out forms, I asked the assistants to fax the forms to me so I could fill them out in advance and fax them back before my appointment. This saved everyone time, and when I got to the doctor's office, I had almost no paperwork to fill out. Besides, my complete medical notes were at home, and I could use the information to help fill in the blanks. I didn't have to rely on fuzzy memories while sitting in the doctor's office trying to reconstruct past history.

■ I always faxed the night before to confirm the next day's appointment time. (This saved me hours of driving due to the inevitable mix-ups between doctors' offices.)

- I always double-checked that referrals from my primary care doctor had been received by the specialists who needed them. This has saved me from several incidents, I believe, of the frustration that comes from showing up at the specialist's door and being told that I couldn't see the doctor because the referral hadn't yet arrived.

I'm sure that the office staffs I dealt with appreciated having information written down. They also had fewer phone calls to answer because we did everything by fax. I faxed information late at night if that was convenient for me. Sometimes, the doctor had actually read the information before I arrived!

DISCOVERING A LOST ART—KEEPING IN TOUCH

Staying in touch and saying thank you are both activities that often get lost in the shuffle of our busy lives. Writing a note by hand happens so seldom these days that personal correspondence from you will make a great impact on the recipient. Of course, this takes time and effort, but there are ways to set up a system to speed the process. Like everything else, writing is a habit that can be acquired with practice.

First, get the supplies you need:

- Purchase a wardrobe of pretty, somber, formal, colorful, and zany cards, notepapers, and stationery.

- If you order paper products, save time by having your return address printed on the envelopes.

YOU'LL THANK YOURSELF LATER

A good rule is to always, always confirm medical appointments before you leave. Making one extra call is worth the few minutes it takes: It could save you hours if your doctor was called away or your appointment is listed for another day.

- Keep a supply of special occasion cards; birthdays, condolences, friendship, and thank yous are just a few you might want on hand.

- If it would inspire you, get different colored pens and markers to go with your stationery.

- Store writing supplies close at hand by your desk or wherever you sit down to write. Or place them all in a basket that you can tote with you to the porch or pool-side.

- If you don't have a place to write, make one.

Writing personal correspondence can be a quick and easy task. A few lines are really all you need to get most messages across. Beautiful prose is not required; genuine feelings are all you need to express. Remember, no one is looking for perfection; it *is* the thought that counts!

Incidentally, Hallmark makes a collection of cards especially designed for business purposes, stating a great case for making a five-minute investment in building stronger relationships. Its "Business Expressions" catalog offers a good-looking selection of cards for almost any purpose: motivating employees, thanking customers, congratulating successes, and networking. Products I thought were clever and especially useful are cards that lend themselves to enclosing newspaper or magazine articles and birthday or congratulations cards that include a music CD.

You can track your correspondence on your computer database (see Chapter 9, "Time-Savers at the Office"), or get Hallmark's "Take Five Organizer" with dividers so

QUICK ⬛ PAINLESS

Keep a stash of different cards at home and you'll never realize that you forgot to send a "thank you" card again!

you can track to whom you've sent cards and for what reason. The organizer also holds a supply of blank cards.

CLEANING

There is cleaning, and then, there is *CLEANING*. In an effort to avoid perfection and keep things moving in your life, I am going to discuss cleaning. Why, you ask? Because it's important we all be reminded that sometimes, we just don't need to worry about dust on the top of the door jambs or the cobwebs in the attic. We have retirement to deal with those issues! Right now, you want a semblance of order and cleanliness, enough to keep the health department away and perhaps even strike a chord of pride about your home—even when visitors drop in unexpectedly.

   As in other areas of your life, prevention is the best medicine. Use these techniques to avoid some dirt in the first place:

- If you can train your children and their friends to take off their shoes when they come in, you'll have made a huge dent in the dirt department. (I won't push my luck and suggest that you advise your grownup guests to do the same.)

- Always use exhaust fans over the stove and in bathrooms.

- Place big doormats outside in front of all doors leading to the inside.

- Put durable, washable scatter rugs in the foyer, mud room, or wherever people tend to enter the house.

IF YOU'RE SO
INCLINED

If you're continually behind in your reading, you "hate" to read, and you put it off dead last on any to-do list, it could be because you're just lousy at it! Admit defeat. Sign up for a speed-reading course or a home study program, maybe even get a tutor. Good reading skills will make a huge impact on the rest of your life—and not just your working life.

- Replace gathered, pleated, dust-catching lampshades with smooth ones.

- Have slipcovers made for your furniture. That way, you can take them off to wash or dry clean.

- Spray everything fabric you own with Scotchguard fabric protector.

- Use dishcloths, rather than sponges, for all clean-up. Fabric cloths can be bleached and washed over and over again. Sponges are magnets for bacteria.

- Make it a rule: no eating anywhere except the kitchen or dining room or wherever you want to keep food crumbs and stains contained.

- Put things away right after you use them. Make a sweep every evening to see that all clutter is cleared.

- Remove some clutter permanently. The more "stuff" on shelves, tables, and counters, the more you've got to dust.

- Display collections behind glass-doored cabinets.

- Keep pets bathed and brushed; they bring in a goodly portion of your home's dirt.

- Confine your pets to the outside or even to just a few rooms or areas in the house.

- Become a fan of aluminum foil: Use it to line the bottom of your oven, roasting pans, and cookie sheets. Rinse it off and recycle it.

Assuming you're not hiring cleaning help, here are some tips for speedy housework:

- Keep all your cleaning supplies together.

QUICK 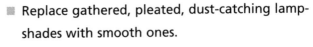 PAINLESS

I love paper towels. Use them in any bathrooms the kids use, and save yourself mountains of dirty towels. You might also find them handy near the work area in the garage and in the play-room and children's rooms if anything wet reaches those locations.

- If you live in a multi-story house, keep a set of supplies on each floor.

- Start from the top and work down.

- Dust first, and then vacuum.

- Tackle cobwebs with a round brush on a long handle made for that purpose, or use a large fluffy sock tied on a broom stick.

- Give walls a swipe occasionally with an all-purpose cleanser in a spray bottle; pay particular attention to light switches and around doorknobs.

- I swear by Clorox Clean Up for white porcelain and tile; spray it on and let it work while you do something else. It works great in the shower, too!

- Soak paper towels with ammonia and place them on wire racks in the closed oven overnight. Oven-cleaning the next day will be a snap.

- Give the refrigerator a quick swipe every couple of days—so much easier than letting it get out of hand. Clear out old food regularly, too.

- Shampoo your carpets yourself with rented equipment. It's inexpensive, and regular cleanings are better for your carpets than ground-in dirt. It's worth a try if you haven't attempted it before....

YOU'LL THANK YOURSELF LATER

When purchasing new furniture, carpeting, and rugs, choose subtly patterned and textured items; they will do a better job of camouflaging dirt than smooth solid fabrics.

Calendaring to Control Cleaning

All of the tips I've given you so far in this chapter are wonderful, but you might be wondering when you'll ever get around to it all. First of all, you won't. You won't do it all at once, that is. The best way, by far, is to spend,

If you're *really* behind with housework and you are desperate, hire a cleaning service to come in for a day and get you caught up. Then, you'll just have to stay kept up.

say, 45 minutes a day on house cleaning. Give yourself a time allotment and stick to it. Your allotment will also act as your time limit and probably motivate you to finish a project on time (and more quickly to boot!). Keeping things clean will never overwhelm you if you keep at it.

When you're in a cleaning mode, don't let interruptions sabotage your efforts. Shoo the kids outside if you can, let the machine pick up the telephone, and keep the front door locked if you tend to get drop-in visitors.

Schedule housework as you do any other chore. As always, establishing a system will help you keep up and take some decision-making out of your life. You won't have to mentally debate whether to tackle the bedroom, you'll simply know whether it's time to do it at all.

Monday evenings, for example, you might schedule for changing bed linens, Wednesday evenings could be laundry night, and Friday morning, you could leave bleach working in the bathrooms. This way, you won't spend your entire weekends cleaning.

Don't forget to enlist the whole family in house-cleaning. The kids should have their jobs listed somewhere, and you *know* they'll willingly and cheerfully rush to get them done. Work out a deal with your spouse.

WARDROBE WONDERS, OR HOW TO FIND TIME IN YOUR CLOSET

I work with many women who are totally confused about their wardrobes and feel badly about the amount of clothes they own. They can no longer fit any new clothes into the closet, they have a lot of clothes they never wear, and they spend much more time than necessary just getting dressed in the morning. (Either that or they spend no time at it and *look* like it!)

Clothing is one area where severe pruning will save hours. My friend Connie has worked out a clothing system that we should all adopt: She has a few good quality, beautiful garments that work together and that she wears until they are tired. It was an eye-opener one day for me to hear her say that she owns only two pair of gym socks! It inspired me to go home and get rid of eight pairs of socks that just sit in my dresser drawer, taking up space. Less is truly more, and there is nothing more liberating than keeping just what you need and no more. (It just goes to show you that we all need coaching in some areas of our lives!)

Carefully read the packing section of Chapter 12, "Tip-Top Travel." Your clothes system at home should not be much more complicated than your routine on the road. Coordinating basic colors with great accessories is the formula.

This simple rule of thumb will result in a wonder wardrobe! Here are some other wardrobe-purging and building ideas:

- Stick with only one color palette so you can buy shoes, bags, and other accessories in only black or navy or taupe.
- As you add items to your wardrobe, look for low-maintenance fabrics and patterns.
- Buy classic pieces.

You've done it! The living room has been stripped of much of its clutter, you've written down a cleaning schedule, and you've got a plan to keep the dirt down to a tolerable level. Buy yourself a big bunch of beautiful flowers to add color and freshness.

The Lazy Way

- If you can't do this yourself, have someone help you put together outfits for you to grab in the mornings so you don't have to think.

- Stay out of stores; save more time.

- Get rid of all but two "painting" or "gardening" or "fishing" outfits.

- Enlist expert help: Get advice and clothes from a direct sales clothing company such as Doncaster. You can put together a classic, high-quality, mix-and-match wardrobe in the space of an hour in the home of one of Doncaster's fashion consultants—a sure way to save time and energy and avoid the agony of shopping. (See Appendix C, "Where to Find It," for more information.)

- Wherever you shop, take a list of what you need and take along what you need to match. You'll save a lot of time returning things because you didn't need them or because they didn't look good together.

Spending the time to get your wardrobe in order will pay big dividends, not only with the time you save, but also with how you look and feel.

GETTING A PROFESSIONAL ORGANIZER IN YOUR LIFE

There are times in the lives of most of us when we are completely overwhelmed by the things we must do, when extraordinary circumstances have slowed us down, when work has been particularly demanding, when an illness has occurred (our own or someone close to us), or

IF YOU'RE SO INCLINED

Spend some money (or ask for a gift), and hire a wardrobe consultant to help you go through your wardrobe. Look in the telephone book or ask friends and relatives for referrals for consultants, personal shoppers, or professional organizers. Once you have the basics of your wardrobe established, you'll find it much easier to deal with getting dressed.

when our children or parents have needed most of our attention. It is at times such as these when we must ask for help: from our families, our friends, our community, or our church. Sometimes, it's more practical to hire a professional to help with specific areas to lighten our load. Obviously, I'm leading up to the subject of professional organizers, a relatively new resource—and one that can make your life infinitely more manageable.

Professional organizers (or organizing consultants) are in business because they have solutions to the problems that are bugging you or holding you back. Lack of time, wasted time, too much stuff, disorder, clutter, not finding things, and not knowing what to keep and what to throw out are common complaints. So many of us don't have the time to step back, think up solutions, or even objectively see the problem. Professional organizers to the rescue!

Here are examples of what professional organizers do. If you've got a problem that isn't listed here, don't worry; there's probably an organizer around to tackle it:

- Set up filing systems.
- Clear clutter.
- Consolidate and organize collections, such as books or toys.
- Edit wardrobes.
- Organize closets.
- Set up record-keeping systems.
- Plan garage and estate sales.
- Pay bills.

QUICK ⬛ PAINLESS

Many people are embarrassed at what their professional organizer might find at their home or office and are *sure* that their mess is the worst the organizer has ever seen. Be assured that professional organizers have seen it all, and "all" is a heck of a lot worse than what you're going to come up with! Besides, the worse it is, the happier organizers are. (It's genetic, and we can't help it.)

- Manage property.

- Sort, arrange, and archive photographs.

- Prepare health-insurance claim forms.

- Do personal shopping.

- Train in computer skills.

- Run errands.

- Set up computerized checkbook management.

- Pack or unpack for moving.

- Establish paper-flow systems.

- Teach time-management techniques.

In addition, organizers often end up serving as coaches to help their clients strengthen their weak areas. A pro can spot when a client needs to delegate more, manage his time better, or track his income more closely. They can work on a limited but ongoing basis to help their clients change old habits or establish some new habits. Another expanded duty of an organizer can be advising on interior design. After clearing the clutter, a home or office often needs some brightening, rearranging, accessorizing, or decorating, and an organizer can be helpful in those areas.

Not all organizers will do all things equally well. Be sure you ask a potential consultant what she considers her area of expertise. Call her references. You might as well hire one who is going to excel in the areas you need most.

QUICK ●□● PAINLESS

Two expectations you should have of a professional organizer: confidentiality and non-judgmental help.

Where do you find a professional organizer? Here's where to look:

- Peruse the Yellow Pages under "Organizing Services—Household and Business."

- Ask friends and relatives for referrals.

- Search the Internet; many organizers have set up Web sites.

- Look in your newspaper's classified ads.

- Your banker, accountant, stockbroker, or attorney might be able to refer you to someone.

- Contact the NAPO (National Organization of Professional Organizers) headquarters for a list of local organizers.

Professional organizers generally will have a conversation with you or make a short visit to your home or office to get an idea of your needs. They will quote you an hourly rate or project fee, depending upon the nature of the work. Rates can vary widely, depending upon the organizer's experience and your geographic location; anything between $35 and $135 an hour is possible. Be clear about what you want to see happen during your time together, and be flexible.

STRESS REDUCTION

Okay, you've got an appointment with an organizer next week, and cleaning help will be here tomorrow. But you might not make it until then: You're overdue on a report at work, the washing machine decided to stop mid-cycle

A COMPLETE WASTE OF TIME

The 3 Worst Ways to Use a Professional Organizer:

1. Book them for longer than five hours; most clients start getting glassy-eyed at about three hours.

2. Be unprepared to make some changes. "Yes, but..." will not get you where you want to go. Take the coaching.

3. Expect them to change your life; only you can change your life. It's up to you to maintain the systems you've set up with your organizer.

If you hire an organizer, do as much throwing out as you possibly can before your appointment. Why pay a consultant to watch you sort through garbage?

last night (with a load of wet towels, of course), the baby feels feverish, and you can't find your son's math book. When the world seems to be caving in on you, try some of these ideas to get a grip:

- Get up or get down. If you've been sitting at your desk winding yourself into a tighter and tighter coil, get up and walk around. If you've been on your feet and you want to collapse, take a few minutes and sit down. Even lie down on the floor and stretch!

- Breathe. Close your eyes and take a few long, slow, deep breaths. Empty your mind. Concentrate on your breathing.

- Exercise. Whether you run off to the gym or run out the door for a walk, there's no healthier way to deal with stress than physical activity.

- Get those endorphins flowing: Cuddle with your kid, your dog, or your cat.

- Go have a cup of coffee, tea, or lunch, or take your vitamin pills.

- Keep a cassette or CD player with earphones in a desk drawer. When things get crazy, put the earphones on and listen to something soothing for a few minutes.

- Find a quiet spot and meditate. Take a 10-minute imagined walk in a beautiful place you create in your mind, noting every gorgeous detail.

- Stand up and stretch—arms slowly above your head, head gently rolling in a circle, bending from the waist, aiming your hands towards your feet, and breathing all the while.

- Look out your window.
- Remind yourself that a hundred years from now, it won't matter.
- Find the funny part in what's going on. Try not to lose your sense of humor.

Preventative Maintenance

You've heard this before, no doubt, but I'd be remiss if I didn't remind you to take care of things—your body foremost among them—preventatively. Nothing will reduce stress and save time more than maintaining what you own, lessening the chance of catastrophic break-downs.

Here are your choices; take your pick:

- Your car stranded on a bridge in rush-hour traffic, or regularly scheduled maintenance?
- Water streaming down the living room wall on Christmas Eve, or that tiny leak fixed in October?
- An ulcer costing time, money, and physical pain, or exercise four times a week?
- A lawsuit, or the shaky step repaired?
- Bare-branched trees in August, or a May consultation with a gardener about those tiny bugs?
- A system crash and lost files, or a computer tune-up twice a year?

IF YOU'RE SO
INCLINED

Remember this: 30 minutes now will save you time and money later! If you have to, make yourself a sign to remind yourself of this simple truth and put it where you'll see it every day.

RENEWING OURSELVES

One of Stephen R. Covey's "Seven Habits" is called "Sharpen the Saw" and points out that taking care of ourselves makes everything else we do possible. A dull saw is highly inefficient and takes more energy than necessary to use; a fatigued body and mind are not going to serve you well. Depletion takes place on several levels—physical, emotional, and intellectual—so renewal needs to happen in those arenas as well.

Replenishing yourself needs to hover in the top 10 percent of your priority list at all times. Make appointments with yourself, and block out time that you treat with utmost respect. Look over the following list; which of the following activities do you need to incorporate into your life?

Getting Fit

Once again, we come back to exercise—as a cathartic stress reliever and a source of energy when you're feeling leaden. P-u-s-h yourself out of your chair and get outside or to the gym, and make the best investment in yourself that you can make.

Physical activity needn't be painful, but you do want to push yourself a bit to get your heart pumping and your muscles warmed up. Some aerobic movement is essential, complemented with muscle building (weights, for example), and stretching to maintain—or regain—flexibility.

A combination of these types of movements for 45 minutes, four times a week, equals only three hours. An

Congratulations! You've incorporated some self-renewal strategies into your routine! Treat yourself to a luxurious bubble bath!

The Lazy Way

investment of three hours out of the 168 hours in a week is pretty rock-bottom—especially considering the payoff in stress reduction, increased mobility and endurance, and long-term health effects. Don't forget that a well-maintained body is more productive, and a rested mind is more creative. Exercise actually saves you time down the road, honest!

If you've been completely inactive for awhile or are aerobically challenged, check with your doctor before leaping off tall buildings. Start slow and steady. Get help. Have a friend walk you through the routines at a gym or take walks with you. Consider hiring a trainer for a couple of sessions to get you on the right track.

As with investing your money, the time to start exercising is *now!*

Tuning In

The emotional and spiritual sides of your life can get severely depleted if you don't pay attention to them. Renewal can happen, but only if you're willing to spend the time necessary. Rest assured, however, that developing all the seemingly "peripheral" areas of your life will only serve to enhance your work and career areas by creating balance.

Relationships will not thrive on neglect! Start by doing things that strengthen your most important relationships; a weekend away with your spouse, a day off with a child, or an office retreat are all investments in the people who matter most to you.

IF YOU'RE SO
INCLINED

If you've got a huge backlog of laundry, ironing, and mending, hire someone to come in one day and get it all done. She or he can iron and mend while the wash is being done. Be sure everything gets put away.

Ignoring your spiritual life can leave you feeling off-center, rudderless. Take the time to go within, to seek silence, and to be—not do. Increase whatever activities deepen your own particular spiritual connection: meditate, read the scriptures, pray, spend time in nature, or attend church. There is nothing like the reminder that we are tiny blips in the perspective of the universe to make our concerns shrink to manageable size!

Turning On

Use your brain to expand your world and give those synapses a workout and challenge. Turn off the TV, stop thinking about work-related dilemmas, and learn something! Read good books, study a language, take a motorcycle apart, or learn the flute. Anything you do will further round out the deprived areas of your life and add to your effectiveness in the other areas.

All this "saw sharpening" might seem like a pleasant but unrealistic dream to you right now. Know that they are all Quadrant II activities (important but not urgent), which I discuss later in the book. But by spending time on these activities, you will not only create a balanced, harmonious life, but also you will find time you never knew you had.

IF YOU'RE SO INCLINED

If you're a big television watcher, the best way to find more time is to get rid of all your TV sets. Guaranteed!

Getting Time on Your Side

	The Old Way	The Lazy Way
Taking your 3 kids to the doctor	3 trips	1 trip
Getting stuck in the waiting room	Hours	No more
Writing personal correspondence	Always meant to…	30 minutes
Cleaning the house	All day Saturday	30 minutes a day
Letting the little stuff get you down	All the time	Never again
Regretting "lost time"	Every day	Never again

Organizing Your Life into Shape

Are You Too Lazy to Read "Organizing Your Life into Shape"?

1 The usual way for you to determine your credit card balance is to call the company; you can never find that bill when it's time to write checks. ☐ yes ☐ no

2 Your idea of "quick banking" is a short line at the bank. ☐ yes ☐ no

3 Your workday starts at 6:30 PM when everyone has left the office and has stopped interrupting you. ☐ yes ☐ no

six

Goals, Lists, Priorities, and Schedules

Managing our lives and getting everything done can be a tough assignment. But stick with this process, and with a bit of effort and thought, you can put *The Lazy Way* to work for you. I'll help you put some structure and systems into place that will, I'm sure, simplify your life. Getting the "big picture" clear will help put the daily, mundane things we all have to do into perspective.

WHAT DO YOU WANT?

In the end, managing your time effectively all comes down to how you want to lead your life. Stopping long enough to sit down and figure out what's important to you might be the most important time-management—and time-saving—exercise you can do. After all, how do you know whether you're spending your time appropriately if you don't have a clear idea of what you want to spend your time doing?

You can do any of the "homework" assignments here in several short sessions. Your brain has a way of working while you're not actively thinking about something, and other objectives, goals, and pieces of your life pie will occur to you after the fact. Feel free to amend your lists!

Kerry Gleeson, in his book, *The Personal Efficiency Program*, puts it this way: "Most of us want happiness in life. But what brings it about? Happiness is a by-product of working and living with meaning and purpose. Establishing goals based on one's values provides that meaning and a purpose for living."

Time-saving tips have their place, but the bottom line is, what are you saving time for? This is why, before we get into speedy solutions, we need a short discussion of your big picture.

And You Thought You Were Too Old for Homework!

I'm going to ask that you invest a little time, with pen and paper, writing down some things later in this chapter. Now is the time to think about the different parts of your life and then to set goals for each part. Don't worry—I give you explicit guidance when we get to that section. Be patient, and put in the time; this exercise will get you where you want to go.

WHERE DO YOU WANT TO GO?

If you figure out what you want to do, where you want to go, and what's important in your life, you're going to save yourself a lot of questions about how to spend your time. You'll probably also feel less frustration knowing that you've made choices and prioritized to keep you pretty much on the right path—the path you've consciously chosen for yourself.

WHAT DOES YOUR LIFE AND DESSERT HAVE IN COMMON?

Think of your life as a pie. The slices of the pie, in different sizes, are the different aspects of your life. A typical "life pie" might be sliced into the following pieces:

- Career
- Family
- Social
- Financial
- Physical
- Spiritual

If you'd like, you can break each piece into more specific pieces. Career, for example, can consist of your current job and professional development—such as the article you're writing on your specialty for publication. Family could be further broken down into Spouse and Children or Spouse and Parents.

You can add and subtract from this list, of course. You might want to add a Personal Development category to your pie; learning French or trekking the Himalayas might be a big piece of your pie. Community or Church might hold great value in your life and might need to stand alone. Whatever the pieces are, write them down.

Your First Assignment

Out with the pen and paper: Block out seven minutes for your first session, sit down, and start writing down the

Congratulations! If you've completed assignment #1, you're well on your way to painting your own "big picture." Because you've been dealing with pie, reward yourself with dessert tonight.

I find these thinking-and-writing assignments much easier to do with a like-minded friend, spouse, or significant other. Recruit someone you trust who also wants to give his life direction, and do it together.

pieces of your personal pie. You can draw a circle and label sections of it, or simply write a list. Think of every part of your life that is important to you. Just let your thoughts flow, and remember, there are no right or wrong ways to do this.

Expect to spend some time with this. Not all of your ideas will come rushing at you in one fell swoop! Change your list as new things occur to you or as you realize you want to eliminate some of the pieces of your pie.

Your Second Assignment

Here's the most challenging part of this book—and the most rewarding if you do it. For each of the pieces of your pie, write down long-term goals for that part of your life. You might think 18 months in the future, 10 years ahead, or your final achievement in any particular area. If you can set goals for all three timeframes, so much the better.

Your goals should be realistic and attainable, but also challenging. Stretch the envelope and aim high. If you're 56 years old, it might not be realistic to establish a goal of becoming a doctor. Conversely, you might want to push yourself harder if your goal is to write one professional article in the next three years.

Know that goals are shifty things; they will change, depending upon your age, your interests, developments at your company and within your family, your health, and a myriad other factors. The important thing is to write down the longest-term goal you can think of now.

Every Goal Gets a Date

It's been said that a goal without a date for attaining it is the definition of a dream—or just a list of good intentions. Write a realistic date next to each goal on your list.

THE ACTION PLAN, STEP BY STEP

The next thing you need is an action plan to chart your course. How are you going to get to your goal by the date you've set? Like mapping out a project, work out the steps to achievement chronologically. And write them down. For every goal you've set, write down the interim steps to attaining it. These steps will be the building blocks of your life.

Being Specific

Both your goals and the interim steps to get to them should be specific. "Get in shape" just isn't a clear enough goal to keep you motivated. It's certainly not measurable: How do you know when you're in shape? Replace "Get in shape" with "Lose 20 pounds by December 31" and "Reduce body fat by 15 percent by June 15." Those goals are clear and concise. It's hard to cheat and easy to know whether you've achieved them.

The interim steps to the get-in-shape goal might be "Work out at gym one hour four times a week, starting now," and "Start Weight Watchers in September."

The preceding steps can be further broken down into your action steps: Call the two gyms you are considering joining and get the membership information or book a

IF YOU'RE SO INCLINED

To help with your goal-setting session, ask yourself this basic question: What would be important if I only had nine months to live? I'm betting the answers to what's important and what you'd like to accomplish will quickly become more apparent.

visit. This way, you'll be getting closer to making those four workout sessions a week.

More Examples

A long-term goal might be "Take my CPA exam." Once you've established a date for completion, the steps of your action plan might include signing up for appropriate educational courses to prepare you for the test. The steps before that might be to gather information on the educational possibilities, timing, and cost to start a course of study to become an accountant. Don't forget to set a deadline for each step.

Break down every goal into small, workable, attainable pieces, and you'll have a road map showing you where you're going and how you're going to get there.

These exercises are hard work and difficult to fit into a busy schedule. The sure way to get at least your first goals and action steps written down is to make an appointment—or appointments—with yourself to get it done.

Of course, the smaller you break down the steps, the easier it will be to accomplish them. A telephone call, for example, is an attainable step in a day—so keep your steps small enough to manage them with relative ease. Try these ideas:

- Go away for a weekend.
- Form a group of like-minded friends and acquaintances to meet once a week for a month.
- Get up an hour earlier every morning to think about your goals and scribble some thoughts about them.

- Take an afternoon off once in a while. Make a pot of tea to keep you fueled and begin.

- Designate one evening a week to turn off the television and work on your goals. You might make a late night of it and work from 9 PM to 11 PM, but what a more constructive way to spend your time than gazing at a talk show!

A CARD GAME

One of the best things you can do to help yourself achieve your goals is to keep them visible—physically in front of you.

My friend Candi tells a story of writing down her goals after taking a self-development course through her employer several years ago. As instructed, she listed 10 goals on index cards, carried them around with her, and glanced at them regularly. She eventually changed purses and left her index cards in the old purse.

Months later, when she retrieved the first purse, she rediscovered her index cards. She was amazed to see that she had accomplished 8 of those 10 goals! It really speaks to writing down and reading your objectives, reminding yourself of your path, and keeping your brain engaged in the right direction.

A sure way to keep your goals foremost in your mind is to keep them in front of you. Here are some ways to keep your list accessible:

- Hang them by the bathroom mirror so you can glance at them while shaving or brushing your teeth.

IF YOU'RE SO INCLINED

Type your goals on the computer and print the list. Shrink the page they're on, and put the page into the front part of your planner. That way, you'll have them with you all day, every day.

- Write them on index cards, as Candi did, and put them into your wallet or purse.
- Put them on your bulletin board in your office.
- Tack them up by your computer.
- Insert your list into a simple frame and hang it on your wall.
- Put your list into your daily planner.

MAKING THE RIGHT CHOICES

By aligning your action plan with your activities and the time you have available, you are generally going to make the right choices. You will consciously—or subconsciously—make decisions that are integrated with your goals. Guess who'll be much further along in achieving his or her goals?

Decision-Making Made Easier

The other benefit of all this hard work is that you will know where and how to spend your time. Having a clear idea of where you want to go will enable you to cut the extraneous activities or wasted energy from your life.

You won't spend inordinate amounts of time wondering whether you should take on a new project, change jobs, move to a new city, or have another baby. If they fit into your action plan to achieve your goals, you'll seriously consider them. If they are exciting or pleasant or interesting avenues to take but don't relate to your plans, you'll have an easier time passing them up.

Go with the Flow

As you know, nothing is sure except change. This applies to your goals as well. Your goal list is meant to be a flexible, living document. Sit down a couple of times a year, and take a look at your short-term steps and your long-term goals. Is everything still looking right? Do your goals excite you? Are all the areas in your life in balance? Do you need to hold back in one area and make a bigger effort in another?

Visualization

Don't worry, I'm not getting weird on you. But consider another technique that can be tremendously helpful in reaching your goals—the practice of visualization. Used by accomplished people in every walk of life, visualization uses your own brainpower to create a wanted result. Athletes use visualization to "see" themselves running over the finish line or batting the ball out of the park. Entrepreneurs "feel" the sensation of signing their first big contracts.

Practice visualization regularly, stopping long enough to see—in slow motion—the results you want, the feelings you will experience, the sounds, the tastes, the whole experience of that moment. Do this as though you were in the moment and actually achieving the goal. Just like looking at the index cards, visualization programs your brain to make it all happen.

A COMPLETE WASTE OF TIME

The 3 Worst Things to Do When Writing Down Your Goals:

1. Fail to be specific.

2. Fail to set a date for completion.

3. Fail to write down the accompanying action steps.

ONE PLUS ONE EQUALS TWO

If you've been diligent about goal-setting, you undoubtedly have run into some conflicts. "No more night meetings"—to fulfill your goal of spending more time with your family—might be at odds with a career goal—"Get promotion next year." A financial goal to "Increase my income 20 percent" might conflict with a community goal to "Run for city council."

Obviously, you're not going to feel good about yourself if you're trying to work toward two or more opposing goals. The stress and frustration inherent in such a situation is a high price to pay.

Choices and Changes

Before you go any further, take some time to fine-tune and re-think your goals. As someone once said, "You can do anything, but you can't do everything." It's time to make choices or changes. A goal in the area of self-development might conflict with a family or career objective. You might have to change the target date of a planned promotion. You might even have to delay a goal indefinitely or until the circumstances in your life support your reaching it.

TURNING ON THE ACTION PLAN

Here's where you get into the nitty-gritty of how you spend your time. Your action plan will tell you what you need to do to achieve your goals and when. Now, you need to further break down the steps you want to take. Here's how to manage an action plan:

- Depending upon how long term your goal is, map out the objectives you want to meet in the next two years, year, or months. Write down specific steps to accomplish them and completion dates to accompany them.

- Write down the steps to take in the next week or month for each goal.

- Every week, make an appointment with yourself to take an action step—something to get you closer to your goal.

- If you're like most of us, you'll leave that action step for Thursday or Friday of the week. The action step you have left to do tomorrow or the next day becomes an important part of your daily to-do list.

- Finally, make your action steps part of today's to-do list. Every day, you can take tiny steps in several areas of your life to whittle away the distance between you and your goal.

Coming to terms with what you want to achieve in your life can be a wonderful opportunity to connect with your spouse or partner. The process of figuring out what's important to you as an individual can open new avenues of conversation and thoughts of a partnership. A bonus just might be bringing the thoughts and values of the two of you into closer alignment.

IT ALL COMES DOWN TO TODAY

What you do today is going to have a tremendous impact on the success you'll experience reaching your goals in

QUICK ⬤ PAINLESS

Don't complain about not having enough time. You have all the time there is and as much time as everyone else on the planet: 24 hours every day. You can choose what you do—and what you don't do—so start enjoying the process!

the future. Here are some examples of the significance of accomplishing seemingly tiny chores:

- Make a phone call to one of three financial planners you want to interview. For example, you might make it today's action item to reach your goal of starting on the right road to ensuring that you will have a specific amount of money in your retirement fund 20 years from now.

- Slide that Spanish language cassette tape into your car's tape player every time you drive, and you will contribute to the future success of your goal to land an assignment in Spain and fulfill your dream of "Live in Europe for a year."

- Spend your Wednesday nights at your church's marriage encounter group with your spouse. You might discover that this could be a tremendous investment in your marriage, yielding a happy 35-year marriage.

- Start writing that book on Texas or tea or extraterrestrials! A book only happens chapter by chapter, so make a schedule! Remember that every word you write is a word closer to a finished book.

Here's How It Works

Let's say that one of your family goals is to take a vacation next June. You probably have written down action steps such as "Make airline, hotel, and car reservations," "Research restaurants," or "Get tickets to *The Lion King*." Several months ahead, you'll start working on these steps, one at a time, prompted by your written

Way to go! You've actually done it: written out the action plans to reach each goal. Give your brain a rest and check out the latest action film.

The Lazy Way

steps in your planner. Your deadline for ordering theater tickets is approaching, and you know that because you've looked ahead in your date book during a planning session. "Order theater tickets" gets added to your daily to-do list.

Rather than arrange a whole trip and many details all at once, you break it down and build on the steps you've already accomplished.

GETTING HELP

If the idea of going through the goal-setting steps and establishing an action plan seems overwhelming, consider getting help. These are tough assignments but crucial to your overall success, health, and finances. Here are some ideas of where to look for assistance:

- Join forces with a friend and help each other. Set dates to get together and faithfully keep your appointments. Use the time together to compare notes back and forth, ask tough questions of each other, and encourage each other. You can also trade times; one week, you do your list together, and the next week, you work on your partner's list.

- Hire a coach, many of whom are trained to help with just this sort of project. Coaches are a new brand of consultant who can be useful in walking you through these steps. Some will have more expertise in the career area of your life, so question them thoroughly and use them for just that part of your goal list.

YOU'LL THANK YOURSELF LATER

All the planning and action steps in the world cannot always meet the challenges of change. Our lives, from month to month, week to week, and day to day—even minute to minute—are in a constant change of flux. Be flexible! Your ability to shift tempo—or even direction—midstream is essential to keeping frustration and stress levels low.

- You might find someone through a low-cost or volunteer business organization such as the Small Business Development Association or support or mentoring groups for small businesses and entrepreneurs.

- Start your own group of friends and business acquaintances. Outline what you're looking for, and conduct a short survey to see whether you can drum up a small group of individuals who are willing to do the work involved and who are capable of supporting each other in this process. You might meet every other week and work with one person per meeting.

Getting Time on Your Side

	The Old Way	**The Lazy Way**
Figuring out what to do today	Never did quite figure that out and it's 6 p.m.	2 minutes after looking at the to-do list
Planning a vacation	Last minute, hours and hours, with only a few expensive choices left	Several months, step-by-step
Responding to your boss's question about where you want to be in five years	Gulp	30 seconds because it's on your goal list
Reaching your savings goal	Geez. Where'd the time go?	Exactly as planned, according to your action steps
Learning French	Again, where'd the time go?	Two years, following the plan you wrote four years ago
Spending time with your family	Missed another Little League game	With few exceptions, just the right amount of time

seven

Planning and Prioritizing Your Way to the Top

Thinking ahead is the key to creating some order in a chaotic world. If you're stumped about how to get Project A done, or when to accomplish Dream 432, planning is crucial to making time to accomplish what you want to in life. Setting priorities is about making decisions—the quicker the better—about what to do first and what's most important.

It's been said that one hour of planning can save you three hours of work. I can't guarantee this particular equation, but there's no doubt that making plans will save you a significant amount of time and greatly increase your chances of completing what you set out to do.

IT'S TIME TO MAKE A PLAN, STAN!

Planning can mean jotting down three items on a grocery list, mapping out a workweek on a calendar, or listing long-term goals and in which years you hope to achieve them.

It can also mean applying for college way before the deadline or ordering Christmas cards in October. You can have a weekly plan, a monthly plan, a 5-year plan, a 10-year plan, or a 20-year plan. When it comes right down to it, the back of an envelope with today's errands scribbled on it can be considered a plan!

Why plan? There are as many answers as there are plans, but the biggest reason is that the world has changed and it is a much more complex place than it used it be. Just surviving requires some degree of planning. Jobs are in flux; the days of keeping one career, working for one company, and collecting that company's retirement benefits are gone. Without that security, we've got to think ahead, and that makes planning essential.

Women, because of their changed status in the world, need to plan. Being a housewife and married to Mr. Wonderful for 40 years is now the exception, not the rule. Women have had to assume financial responsibility—voluntarily or not—worry about their own careers and retirements, and generally think ahead. Planning, again, is the cornerstone to a friendly future.

The complexity of our society has made simple things complicated! Time constraints, a lot of people, and ludicrously rapid communication conspire to make our lives

YOU'LL THANK YOURSELF LATER

Planning makes the difference between you proactively controlling your time and passively letting events control your time. Increase your awareness regarding who or what is in control—you or the world around you?

complicated. Think, for example, of the simple act of going out to dinner. It's not so simple any more when the criteria are that you only have Friday night free this week, the place is getting rave reviews and is deemed the "hottest" spot in town, and everybody wants to try it. Try to dine there without the step called planning!

The concept of "drop in" seems doomed. The barber, the doctor, your insurance lady, and even your child's teacher aren't sitting around waiting for you to come by. They are all so busy that they require an appointment. Just try to see a dentist without an appointment! Life demands that we plan ahead.

The good news about planning, however, is that it provides a step-by-step guide to accomplishing your action steps, eventually leading to your long-term goals. Sitting down and charting a plan creates a road map, if you will, to point you in the direction you want to go and to keep you on track. To plan is to control the course of events, rather than let events control you. This daily investment of your time will reap so many rewards.

However far you've taken your own planning, here are some basic tips to make the most of this practice:

- Planning requires an investment in time up front. Where do you think the expression "plan ahead" came from? Not planning pretty much guarantees that you'll be wasting time and creating crises.

- Make up a weekly plan, based on the appointments you have already booked. To those, you will add one, or several, action steps that you've decided will enable you to reach your long-term goals. This step

QUICK PAINLESS

Get up 30 to 60 minutes earlier to plan and organize your day or week. That quiet time is a perfect opportunity to think ahead with a clear, unfrazzled mind.

will keep you in touch with your long-term goals and the big picture.

- Ideally, you will plan every day. You'll update today's plan, look over your planned week, and scan the month ahead. Take one percent of your day for planning and control the remaining 99 percent. Not sure how to accomplish this? Read on!

TWEAK YOUR DAY, EVERY DAY

Start by setting aside 15 minutes last thing before you stop working in the evening to see what tomorrow brings and what you want to accomplish. Look in your planner and see what's scheduled. This will help you prepare mentally for whatever is ahead and will serve as a good reminder in case you need to prepare something in the morning for an activity in the afternoon. If you've got to take cookies to school at 2:00 p.m., you'll want to wake up knowing you've got to bake a batch or make a trip to the store.

Looking Ahead

Once a day, look ahead at the next few days. On Thursday afternoon or Friday morning, turn to the next week. Should anything be shifted so that you can use your time more efficiently? Are tasks grouped physically together? For example, are your sales calls all in one area of town? Are all your meetings close by, or can you make some adjustments to see that they are?

Looking several days ahead of schedule allows ample time for you to shuffle things around and see whether

QUICK **n** PAINLESS

You might try making today's plan based on a weekly plan. If you can see your week's objectives in front of you, you'll be able to break them down into bits and pieces and make up your daily plan from these.

another plan will work better for you. This is when you might be able to call two people to your office rather than meet with them separately about the same issues. You might need a couple of weeks to cancel two trips to Dallas if you can fit all of your meetings into one trip at another time.

Although some days, it might seem that you don't even have the time to make another phone call, it's truly worth the time if you can save a couple of hours or days in exchange for the investment you made planning.

Making All the Pieces Fit

Now, look at what isn't scheduled in your planner. Study your to-do list, and ask yourself what still needs to be done that can be fit into any empty slots you see ahead:

- Fit a short piece of a long-term project into your day.

- Fill in a narrow gap in the schedule with something you'd rather not do (cold calls, for example).

- You have a business meeting near your child's school. Schedule the meeting for around 2 p.m. and be there to pick up your child when school gets out. (Then, indulge in ice cream cones!)

- Make an appointment with yourself to go to the library and do some research on the book you're writing.

- You notice that the trade show you're attending next Wednesday is in your client's neighborhood; perhaps you can schedule a short meeting with her.

YOU'LL THANK YOURSELF LATER

Some folks start their mornings with a short planning session while their minds are fresh and their energy high. Don't let the day intrude on you before you've spent the time necessary to plan. Get up early or make yourself unavailable to keep this time sacred.

Way to go! You've made a weekly plan and a daily plan—a great beginning. Book a doubles game with your tennis buddies.

The Lazy Way

Once you've decided how you're going to fill a gap, write down that activity, even if it doesn't involve anyone other than you (such as going to the gym). Writing it down as though it were an appointment makes it more likely to happen. Fitting in a task between two appointments, with a deadline staring you in the face, will help you focus and work efficiently. And it will give the unpleasant tasks a short timeframe.

PLANNING FOR FUN

The final piece of daily planning is to look at where you can fit in some fun. Remember why you're managing your time? Not every second needs to be filled with activity. Presumably, you want more seconds filled with pleasurable activities. You don't have to fill in all the gaps with work-related chores. Here are some ways to keep some fun in your life:

- Free for lunch? Call your spouse, a good friend, or a good customer and make that lunch a good one.
- Can you leave early to hit some golf balls and get some fresh air?
- Can you take a break, hit the gym, or have a jog and get back in time for your 4:00 meeting?
- Can you disappear to the library and finish that mystery that's keeping you up late at night?

PRIORITIES

So you know what you need to do. You have your main long-term objectives in mind. You also have your short-term goals guiding your behavior—most of the time. You have projects, people, paper, and money to juggle. It's a tough job deciding what to do first and who or what takes precedence, so let's look at some alternative ways to do this.

As Easy as A, B, C

Write down each task on a card and spread them out on your desk. Make piles of A, B, and C tasks, where A is the most important. Of course, they're all important, but shuffle the absolutely most important to the A list. With long-term objectives in mind, you'll eventually be able to divide the rest of the cards into the B and C stacks.

Another way to do this is to write a list of all your to-dos and mark them A, B, and C. Everyday, during your planning interlude, make your daily to-do lists reflect A's and B's.

One way to think about your list is to name them as follows:

- A: Must do
- B: Should do
- C: Could do

Fine-Tuning Your ABC's

You can further break down your ABC's if that would help you think more clearly about your priorities. Divide the items marked A into three levels—A1 for top priority, and then A2, and finally A3. Do the same with your B and C items.

IF YOU'RE SO INCLINED

Glancing at your week—whether it's on paper or your computer calendar—is a good visual clue to how you are managing your time. Step back further and get an even bigger picture by looking at your activities on a monthly calendar. You can do this most easily by using a computer calendar program.

Ann McGee-Cooper and Duane Trammell have a great suggestion in *Time Management for Unmanageable People.* They suggest that you write each to-do on different colored sticky notes. Place the notes on a clear plastic clipboard with the most important ones placed highest. Set it on your desk, visible above the clutter, and you will always have your planned activities in front of you. Even better, you can shift the sticky notes around according to your mood or changes in priorities.

Colorize as You Prioritize

Another way to more graphically see what needs to be done is to put each A item on an index card or sticky note. Put all the B's on a card or note of another color. Add a third color for your C's. Now, place your cards on a table and rearrange, if necessary, change colors, or further prioritize them with A's, B's, and C's.

Taking the time to establish a hierarchy might make it clearer at a glance what needs to be done next, saving you "think time" between projects, keeping you productive at a uniform rate, and keeping your momentum up.

The best way to keep lists of your long-term goals, interim action steps, and to-do list is to enter them in the computer. You can easily remove, adjust, and add to each of your lists and print the latest version. Bring action steps further forward as necessary and to-dos to the top of the list when appropriate. File any previous lists, or keep them in a binder, so you can occasionally check your progress.

THE 20/80 THEORY

A hundred years ago, an Italian economist by the name of Vilfredo Pareto (1848–1923) developed what is called the Pareto Law, or the 80/20 Rule. He figured out that 20 percent of the population in 19th century England enjoyed 80 percent of the wealth of that country. Further study revealed that the same pattern repeated itself consistently when he examined different countries and different time periods. Every example he chose mathematically came out with the same results.

Others took up the study of this relationship and determined that 20 percent of any resource—such as people, time, or skills—result in 70 to 80 percent of the productivity of that resource.

For example, 80 percent of corporate profits are generated by only 20 percent of the products. There are literally thousands of ways to illustrate how this principal works, but in the context of time management, let's take a look at how 20 percent is responsible for 80 percent.

Pareto's Law states that 80 percent of your accomplishments are achieved in 20 percent of your time. If that's true, it might mean that 80 percent of our time is not particularly productive and that we just have to worry about maximizing 20 percent of our time! Now, doesn't that take the pressure off, knowing you only have to worry about 20 percent?

Think about your own life and how you spend your time. Does it fit? Can you make a case for the 80/20 Rule in your own experience? Here are some earth-shattering beliefs regarding time shared by the disciples of Pareto:

IF YOU'RE SO
INCLINED

If you use an electronic organizer, it's a good place to keep your lists; it can store your long-term goals and keep the to-do list handy.

- We only use our time well 20 percent of the time.

- If we double our efforts on the most productive 20 percent of our activities, we still have 60 percent "free time" and have doubled our productivity.

- Another way of putting this is that the most productive time on a project is often the last 20 percent (you know—that burst of energy to meet a deadline). If we gave ourselves half the time to complete a project, doesn't it stand to reason that we might accomplish things in half the time?

When planning, always allow extra time for unforeseen delays. Surprises show up in the form of no cabs in a rainstorm, the copier running out of paper, or your boss asking for a rush job. Always allow some breathing room between activities.

If this is making sense to you, here's a brief outline of how to apply the 80/20 Rule to your own life:

1. Sit down—spend as much time as you need—and determine what 20 percent of your activities is responsible for 80 percent of your money, your sales, your happiness, or your productivity. This is the key step you need to take to apply the 80/20 Rule.

2. When you've done the first step, you should have a good sense of what you are best at—those activities that get the "juices flowing" in your life, that bring you satisfaction and success.

3. Then, concentrate on the 20 percent. How can you increase those activities that have already generated so much? Set a goal for yourself to raise the 20 percent to 30 or 40 percent within a year or 18 months.

Don't forget, either, that some of the 80 percent you spend doing low-achievement activities can be jettisoned. They might never be missed! If you're concentrating on your productive 20 or 30 or 40 percent, it will be easy to let the low-value activities drop by the wayside.

URGENT DOES NOT MEAN IMPORTANT

When planning your time, keep one important concept in mind: What is urgent is not always important. Stephen R. Covey, who wrote *The 7 Habits of Highly Effective People*, taught me a valuable lesson with his "Time Management Matrix." He divides everything we do into four quadrants. I'm willing to bet that his concept will make you rethink your priorities. Here's how he has categorized the kinds of things we do that take up our time:

- Important and urgent
- Important and not urgent
- Not important and urgent
- Not important and not urgent

Here are some examples of what these different quadrants represent:

- **Quadrant I: Important and urgent:** The house is burning, a proposal is due next week, your presentation to the city council is scheduled for Thursday, and your child is waiting on line 2.

- **Quadrant II: Important and not urgent:** Getting your will updated, leisure activities, strategizing and think time, planning, writing your novel, exercise, and building both personal and professional relationships.

- **Quadrant III: Not important and urgent:** Some meetings, some phone calls, and interruptions. Running to the post office to get a bill paid on time will turn a normal maintenance chore into a real time-waster in this category.

- **Quadrant IV: Not important and not urgent:** Watching television, answering some phone calls, reading catalogs, surfing the Internet, and watching some movies.

Think about which quadrant describes the way you spend most of your time. Obviously, if you're in Quadrant I

QUICK ◖▮▮◗ *PAINLESS*

When it comes to deciding whether something belongs in quadrant one, put your family there first and everything else will stay in perspective!

The 3 Worst Ways to Set Your Priorities:

1. Allowing other peoples' important issues to become your urgent items.

2. Listing too many chores on the A1 list.

3. Forgetting to look at the big picture—your long-term goals.

most of the time, you're going to burn out quickly and probably won't accomplish a lot. You're also at a high risk of getting sick due to the level of stress you endure by continually putting out fires.

Living in Quadrant III also involves a lot of stress and wasted energy spent on doing the wrong things. A Quadrant III person often does things that are important to others.

Anyone in Quadrant IV is probably not a productive person and might claim a long list of failures and a short list of accomplishments.

Your aim is to be in Quadrant II as much of the time as possible—thinking and planning ahead, taking care of yourself, following through, and meeting your commitments. A simple example of a Quadrant II activity is having a yearly medical checkup. It's not urgent, but—in the context of your whole life—it is certainly one of the most time-saving things you can do and an activity that could prevent a crisis from erupting.

The Impossible Dream?

The key to getting things done in Quadrant II is to schedule them. Making time for these activities will enhance your life, lend balance, enrich your relationships, and help your career and intellectual development. They simply won't happen by themselves, and you'll need to be pretty stern and disciplined with yourself to keep these activities high on your priority list.

The following is just a list of Quadrant II possibilities that can—and should be—scheduled into your life.

Anything else you want to accomplish—your wildest dreams and the fun stuff—should be included on your list to work into your planning:

- Working on the great American novel, working in your wood shop, or training your goldfish to sing. Make room for your passion.

- Exercise four times a week. You know it's the only way.

- Reading time, both for work and pleasure.

- Planning time every morning or evening. Even if it's only 10 minutes, glance at tomorrow's activities and the rest of the week.

- Office or home organizing (twice a year or in short, quick bursts).

- Book the massages or the photography lessons you promised yourself; put them down as though they were business meetings. Treat them with the same importance.

- Continuing education and self-development classes.

- Update your will.

- Play time. Vacations.

- Do absolutely nothing.

PRODUCTIVE CYCLES

Most of us have certain times of the day when we're likely to take on the world and leap from tall buildings. If you're like most of us, you also have a daily period—or more—when you're dragging a bit and not at the top of

Good going. You've actually crossed a few things off your to-do list. Get out and share a latte with a friend.

The Lazy Way

your game. Analyze your daily rhythm and see whether you can define what times of the day are your most productive.

You might want to literally track your alertness levels for a few days; paying attention to your own rhythm might be an eye-opener for you. Assess each hour of the day and rate your energy level from 1 to 5, with 1 being your lowest level. See if you can't identify a pattern in when your 1's and 5's show up during the day. If you can, use that information to help you decide how you schedule your activities.

The trick here, of course, is to maximize your productive periods by licking the hard jobs during those times. You want to maximize your number 5 periods and use them to the fullest. During your most productive peaks of the day, you want to schedule the following:

- Do the hardest job on your to-do list.
- Work with figures and numbers.
- Solve problems.
- Write, if that's a hard task for you.
- Deal with unpleasant people (so you have high energy and make your interactions with them go quickly!).

Tackling these jobs when your energy is low is probably going to take more time that it would if you were alert. You'll also make more mistakes. Scheduling your most challenging tasks for your "up" times will result not only in accomplishing more, but also in doing a better job.

IF YOU'RE SO INCLINED

Have a few C projects been on your to-do lists for months? Consider not doing them. If they really were important, they'd have been given a higher priority and would have been started or even finished by now.

Here are some of the things you can put off for those low-energy times of your day:

- Return phone calls.
- Iron.
- Read journals and the newspaper.
- Sit down and read to your child.
- Take a walk around the block.
- Respond to email.
- Organize a drawer.
- Put papers into their assigned binders.
- Start dinner.
- File.
- Take a nap.

Whatever you do, to the extent that this is possible, don't fight your natural rhythms. A body and mind can only give so much peak performance! If you're struggling, pay attention to what your mind is telling you. Stop. Find something else to do. Take a break.

Good for you! You figured out that you're totally useless at 4 p.m. every day. Take that time and—without guilt—have a latte, take a brisk walk, or browse your favorite bookstore.

The Lazy Way

Getting Time on Your Side

	The Old Way	The Lazy Way
Forgetting to get something done	All the time	Never again!
Running out of time	Every day	Never again!
Running in circles	All day	Not any more!
Finding time for fun	I don't even have time for the stuff I have to do!	I planned for it!
Having a whole day blown by one delay	All the time	Never again!
Keeping your priorities straight	Help me!	Got it!

Chapter
eight

Using a Planner

I think the single most important habit you can adopt to help you manage your time better is to use a paper planner, organizer, or calendar. Call it what you will; this is the single most valuable tool you can use to keep your head above water, to manage your time, to keep yourself on track, and to plan ahead for the future—whether that's tomorrow, next month, or next year. There are many high-tech calendaring systems to choose from, but to get started *The Lazy Way*, a paper system is the way to jump-start your time-management education.

Some other significant advantages of using a paper planning system is that it's always accessible (as long as you don't lose it), you don't need electricity or batteries to use it, a power surge won't affect your data, and it's inexpensive.

BEYOND APPOINTMENTS

Planners are not only a place to write appointments, but also offer you a visual cue to where your time is going and how to best manage it. Properly used, your planner can help you

- Consolidate tasks efficiently
- Break down projects into manageable small steps
- Keep you on top of important relationships
- Help you follow through with promises and commitments

THE CHOICES

There are several excellent manufacturers of well-thought-out organizing systems on the market. Do some research at your local stationers or office supply stores, and look over the assortments available. Check out Appendix C, "Where to Find It," to find information on ordering catalogs from the companies listed in the following sections.

Day-Timers, Inc.

Day-Timers originated the personal planner in 1947 and offers a huge line of paper planners, planning software, leather goods, personalized stationery, and management training programs. Day-Timers come in virtually every size and configuration; its experience in this field is evident in the way its functional products are designed.

FranklinCovey

FranklinCovey is a merger of Stephen Covey's Leadership Center and Franklin Quest. Stephen R. Covey is one of this country's foremost management experts and author of, among other titles, *The 7 Habits of Highly Effective People*. Franklin planners have been around for generations. FranklinCovey offers planning systems of every

YOU'LL THANK YOURSELF LATER

Yet another Golden Rule: Use only one planner. Just one. I've seen too many clients courting disaster because their "other" planner isn't with them. Trust me on this one. As with all rules, there is an exception to this one, but only one, and I get to that in Chapter 11.

type, leather goods, serious time-management tools, and seminars. You can find standard planner pages and those designed specifically to support the time-management activities taught by Covey.

Day Runner

Day Runner products appear in most office-supply stores and stationers. They are affordable and come in a wide variety of configurations to accommodate almost everyone—from students to homemakers to executives. Their planners are well designed and have coordinated accessories—such as an insert that holds your checkbook, a credit card holder, and even a small light you can snap into your binder—for their many sizes of planners.

Levenger

Levenger puts out a catalog that offers products for "serious readers" and also sells an organizing system called Circa. Not bound and having no binder rings, Circa pages are punched with small notches on their left sides and are held together with round plastic disks. Pages can be "peeled" out and pressed back in the binder at will. You can put different sized pages into the same binder, making it a highly flexible system. Circa refill pages are attractive and simply designed on high-quality paper.

The At-A-Glance Group

The At-A-Glance Group produces a wonderful array of organizing products. With the philosophy that everyone's needs are different, their products reflect the various work styles of different personalities.

QUICK PAINLESS

Before you buy a planner, sit down and think about what you need. Don't spend money on a planner designed for a financial executive if you're a book illustrator.

QuickNotes

QuickNotes are a special line of planners and calendars that use blue and yellow colors for visibility. It's not only attractive, but also helps to visually organize your activities.

LifeLinks

The LifeLinks line is a whole series of "life organizing" products, covering issues well beyond the scope of career-related activities. Their planners have sections for personal, work, and family activities. Read about more LifeLinks products in Chapter 11.

Spiegel Calendar Books

Spiegel calendar books are fine quality, German-made appointment books that have been sold in Europe for 15 years. They are bound books in a handy 6"×8" size, containing fine two-color printed pages and a choice of covers. Two elegant—and practical—touches are the two ribbon markers bound into the book's spine and the perforated corner on each page for locating the current day quickly.

TAKING IT ON THE ROAD

What's important, I believe, is that your planner is portable. Everyone's definition of portable varies, but carrying your planner with you will pay big dividends. You need to have it with you at all times during your day to refer to it frequently. Unless you're one of today's privileged few with a secretary to arrange your scheduling for you, you need your planner with you to make appointments on the run. Otherwise, you often end up having to return to your office, checking your calendar, and making an additional telephone call to set a date.

Your choice of cover for your planner can enhance the portability: Many have wrist straps or shoulder straps.

Size Matters

After portability is the issue of page size. Again, your needs will be unique to your life and activities, but you'll need enough room to at least write down appointments, deadlines, and notes to yourself. The most common sizes for planners are pocket size, with approximately 3"×5" pages. Two handy middle sizes are approximately 4"×6" and 5"×8." The next size up has standard $8\frac{1}{2}$"×11" pages.

Set Up Your Day One Page at a Time

After you've determined how large or small your planner is going to be, you have to figure out how your pages are going to be configured. (Stick with me; this really isn't as complicated as it sounds!)

YOU'LL THANK YOURSELF LATER

I recommend that you get a cover with either a snap or a zipper to keep your planner closed in case it gets dropped or you're wandering around in the rain. Keeping it closed flat will help protect its pages, and you'll be less likely to lose any loose bits and pieces that invariably find their way into a planner.

- A whole month printed on two small pages might be adequate for you. That means you'll only have a small square in which to write the day's activities, which is fine if you have just one or two activities you need to track per day. This kind of calendar can be great for frequent travelers who can line out whole weeks or other periods of time when they'll be on the road. Having a visual picture of your month helps you plan other trips and lets you see where you have the opportunity to get things done while you're at home.

- The next configuration is a week on two pages. This format will allow you to get an overview of your whole week and visually clue you to where there are slots to fill and where times are heavily booked. You end up with approximately one fourth of your page on which to write a day's appointments and headlines.

- If you keep copious notes or billing information in your planner, one page per day might work best for you. A whole page will allow you to list several tightly scheduled appointments and will generally let you have enough room to accommodate scribbles of any kind.

STRIPPED-DOWN VERSION OR CUSTOM OPTIONS?

The third element to consider when putting together a planner is whether you can live with a book-bound or wire-bound book or you need a loose-leaf type that can be customized. The wire-bound types generally lie flatter, but you're limited to what's already bound into the book. Binders with loose-leaf pages let you be creative and make it easy to customize the types of pages you need to make your calendar a real workhorse.

THE CUSTOM TOUCH

There are so many planner options available today that you should be able to customize a system that works

exactly to your specifications. Here are some add-ons, besides the dated pages, that you might find handy and that can be put into a planner with rings:

- Address book
- Clear vinyl pouch for small stuff, such as stamps and coins
- Expense tracking pages
- Auto mileage records
- Meeting agenda
- Project pages
- Blank pages
- Shopping lists
- Toll call record
- To-do lists
- Contact sheets
- Conversation log
- Client information sheets
- Maps
- Voice-mail record
- Clear plastic sheet protectors to hold photographs, business cards, and floppy disks
- Calculator designed to fit on binder rings
- Paper punch to make adding pages to your binder a snap
- Duplicate note pad, such as the one Day-Timer makes; how handy to scribble a note to someone and keep a copy of it yourself!

YOU'LL THANK YOURSELF LATER

Be sure to properly mark your planner with your name and telephone number in case you misplace it. You might have a better chance of getting it back if you mention the word "reward." (I printed a brightly colored page with my identifying information, laminated it, and then stuck it into my planner. Thank goodness I've yet to lose my "bible.")

Make Your Own

To further customize your planner, use blank pages made for your system. Extra pages can be ruled, grid patterned, or plain. With a set of blank binder tabs, you can divide sections for projects, contacts, notes, or anything else you need handy. Both divider tabs and extra pages are often available in colors, so use them to make even speedier work of finding what you need.

Putting Your Book Behind Covers

You can find covers and binders of virtually every material to house your planner, from inexpensive vinyl to fine leather and from space-age fabrics to lovely floral tapestry. Look carefully at handles and straps if you're planning to carry the planner by itself.

Women who'd rather not cart both a purse and a planner can place their organizers into leather purse-like binders with shoulder straps. Both men and women can carry their planners in zippered carryalls that will also accommodate reading material, a file or two, and daily essentials. These are often available in canvas or tough nylon fabrics and have handles or shoulder straps. At-A-Glance's LifeLinks makes a purse/organizer combination.

ALL-IN-ONE

To make an organizer binder more of a purse, you can add several accessories to your binder to increase its usefulness and help you avoid carrying a separate purse:

- Coin case
- Checkbook holder

YOU'LL THANK YOURSELF LATER

If you bought a planning system "preloaded," so to speak, with several sections, take out the parts that you're not going to use. You don't want to cart around an ounce more than necessary!

- Credit card holder
- Mirror
- Calculator

Keep It Light

You can further personalize your organizer with "theme" pages offered by planner manufacturers:

- Day-Timers has beautiful pages with color photo images as backgrounds. They have golf and nature scenes and offer a "Pink Ribbon" planner set, which helps support breast cancer research.

- FranklinCovey sells planner pages that have elegant borders, subtle nature scenes, or feminine designs of pastel floral pages.

- DayRunners has organizer sets and refills with funny "Dilbert" and "The Far Side" themes.

- At-A-Glance has product lines featuring Life, Mickey Mouse, and Millennium collections.

Hi-Tech Techniques

There are many ways to use computers to create the calendars you purchase in paper form. What kind of software you choose will depend on the type of computer you have, your computer skills, and what calendar format you need. Here's what most software programs will allow you to do:

- Enter information that you can instantly print or view in several ways: a day at a time, the week, or a whole month.

Jot reminders to yourself on sticky notes and place them in your planner. If you don't get the item done or the call made this week, move the note to next week. You can also use Levenger's Circa system; jot your note on a small Pocket Note and snap it between any two pages of your planner. Either method will save you from writing and rewriting the same information over and over.

- Color code different types of activities.
- Assign different activities with different priorities.
- Enter recurring appointments throughout a whole year with the touch of a button.
- Create a daily to-do list.
- Store unlimited names and addresses.
- Update with new information easily.
- Print pages in the exact size and format you need.

Computer-generated calendars are not for everyone in that they require a fair amount of computer experience to organize properly. Nor are they generally portable, so they're best used if you have access to your computer all day long. Those of you who meet those criteria might find that electronic calendaring is the way to go.

HANG ON FOR HISTORY'S SAKE

Keep old planners. You might need to hold on to them indefinitely if they are part of your income tax documentation, and you might find it handy to check back occasionally to see what happened when in the past. If your planner is buried with old tax information, you might have a tough time retrieving it.

NOW WHAT?

Okay, you're all set. You've got your planner in front of you, shiny new and pristine. Think of your relationship with your planner as a good marriage: you're in this together, you're gonna stick by it, and you'll pay attention to it. In return, you will derive wonderful benefits and your life will be greatly enhanced. Here are some ways to use your planner to maximize its effectiveness.

How Long an Appointment Really Takes

Appointments are the most obvious items to jot in your planner. But there's a right and wrong way to plan an activity. Here's where we all get into trouble: not allowing enough time for appointments. Rarely is a one-hour appointment one hour! Every date you set needs a "buffer zone" before and after it. Here's why:

- You spend a couple of minutes confirming your appointment.

- Gathering the materials you need can be a step before an appointment.

- Getting there—and that might include getting lost—is something you need to plan.

- The person you're meeting is stuck on a conference call and is eight minutes late.

- Schmoozing afterward or running up to the next floor to meet the company's decision-maker might happen spontaneously and will take more time.

- Someone might ask you to lunch!

- Then, you've got to get back to the office; it might be rush hour by then and you might have to wait for a cab or sit in traffic for 20 minutes.

So a one-hour appointment, out of your office, starting at 10:00 a.m., can translate into a block of your time

You've done it. You've purchased and organized a portable planner system. Now, book yourself a massage and write the time on your calendar.

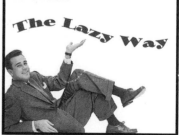

from 9:15 through 11:45. That one-hour appointment takes two-and-a-half hours. It's that extra hour and a half you "lost" that is making your life crazy and keeping your adrenaline pumping too hard and often. This is why you run late. This is why everything takes longer than it *ought* to. This is why you're stressed.

Rule Number One

Rule number one is to block out enough time. Be realistic and generous about how much "extra" time to allocate per activity. This practice will leave you, I promise, with a little "breathing room" and better mental health.

Should you not need all the time you've planned, and you find yourself back at the office at 11:00 a.m., you get bonus time—time to return phone calls, fill out your expense report, take a walk, make notes from your meeting, or update your database.

Plotting Projects

The next things you write in your planner are, funnily enough, plans. This can mean deadlines. It can mean the steps of a project until completion. If the steps are written down, your time line will follow you around, staring you in the face, giving you a much better chance of coming through on time. Once again, *padding* your time needs—allowing for the unexpected—is essential.

The Step-by-Step Method

Let's say you've got a lengthy report due in a month. It will involve getting some figures from the research department for you to incorporate into your report.

Here's how you might map out this "pretend project," noting every step in your planner:

- Start from the due date and work backwards. Enter the completion date in your planner.

- The day you receive the assignment, call the research department to let it know what you'll need and when. You should make notations in your planner of every step you need to accomplish along the way.

- Three days after the start date, the outline of your report should be complete. The research department should receive a confirming note or email about what you've already requested.

- A week later, the research department should have a reminder from you. The first half of the report should be completed.

- Two weeks before due date, you should have the entire first draft complete. You should have received research figures and incorporated them into your report.

- A week before due date, final revisions should be ready for typing.

- Two days before due date, you should be making copies and having the reports bound. If all things have gone according to plan, you could be finished at this point.

- The morning your report is due, you calmly deliver it and feel good about yourself.

Congratulations! You did a great job mapping out your project and completing everything on time without breaking a sweat. Take the research person who helped you out to lunch.

The Lazy Way

How to Make It Fun

Don't laugh. You want to enjoy using your planner, and there are ways to make it fun to use. Any embellishments you make will undoubtedly make it easier to use as well. Here are some ways:

- Make up your own "color code." Using highlighters or different colored pens, mark different activities. You can highlight the writing or draw a colored box around it.

- Draw a colorful streak through days to signal a particular kind of activity: the days you'll be traveling, for example.

- How does the idea of colored dot stickers appeal to you? You can "dot" different activities in the same way you used a highlighter. (You probably have to love polka dots to use this method.)

- Speaking of stickers, you can use little ones of hearts, stars, balloons, airplanes, and so on to liven up your planner.

IF YOU'RE SO
INCLINED

Color-code your planner. Use highlighters or different colored pens to identify different activities. I write all birthdays in colored ink. Some people highlight family activities in one color or each appointment of each family member in a different color to keep it all straight.

Getting Time on Your Side

	The Old Way	The Lazy Way
Finding your next dentist appointment	17 minutes (calling the office to ask)	1 minute
Figuring out when that personnel report is due	1 hour	2 minutes
Making an appointment	2 hours (you didn't have your calendar with you)	39 seconds
Looking up directions to your next meeting	30 minutes	1 minute (they're written in your planner)
Finding out when your sister's birthday is	20 minutes (calling your brother to ask)	30 seconds
How much time you block out in your planner for a one-hour appointment	1 hour	2 hours (including cushion time)

Chapter nine

Time-Savers at the Office

For many of us, our home away from home is the office. The key to being more productive in it—and getting out of it regularly—is to set it up to maximize your efforts during the time you spend there. Think of your office as a battlefield where you wage the war on the avalanche of paperwork that hits you every day of the week. You need to be a carefully prepared soldier!

Check out Chapter 10, "Time-Savers at Home," for a rundown of the bare-bones minimum requirements to set up an office. For more professional needs, keep reading.

There are two issues to consider about your office: organization and neatness. They are not the same thing! If you stop to think about it, you can have a neat and tidy office but still be unable to find what you need when you need it, which indicates a lack of organization. An organized person can sometimes function in a messy environment but probably wouldn't want to for long.

Some incredibly creative personality types can be productive in a chaotically jumbled environment. Whichever type you

On your own or with the help of a consultant, *feng-shui* your office. This centuries-old Chinese art of arranging your living or work space to accommodate and direct energy flow is thought to bring tranquility, wealth, and productiveness to your life. Don't laugh: Highly successful business leaders incorporate *feng shui* practices into their environments. Check it out!

are, you probably need a moderate amount of neatness and more than a little organization in order to function in top form.

MILES OF PILES

Here's a test for you: How much clear workspace can you find on your desk? If less than 50 percent of your desktop or work surface is free, you need to either clear the decks or add more workspace. As always, the less you have, the less you have to organize.

Start a subtraction process:

■ The most important step, once again, is throwing out. Go through everything that's in sight and purge at least half of it.

■ Tear articles from magazines and periodicals and put them in a "To Read" file.

■ Empty shelves and other surfaces of knickknacks that invariably collect; take them home or toss them.

■ Photographs and awards are great, but just a couple of each, please. Edit, edit, edit!

■ Make piles of borrowed things and return them to their rightful owners.

■ Make another pile of things that must be brought home.

■ If you happen to have three chairs in your office besides your own and you rarely have more than one visitor, take out the two extras.

■ How many old computer manuals and instruction booklets do you have lying around? Get rid of them.

- Make this a priority: Go through your files in file cabinets and heavily edit them. Studies have shown that 90 percent of what goes into filing cabinets never gets looked at again. Why are we so adamant about hanging on to everything for so long, I wonder?

- To further reduce the paper around you once you've emptied your files of tossable paper, pull all old materials that you must hang on to and file them in banker's boxes. These are the foldable cardboard boxes that can accommodate both legal and letter-size file folders. If your storage site is at all damp, put your folders into plastic boxes instead. Stash the boxes out of your office, but be sure to label all boxes clearly and in detail.

- Does the water dispenser have to be in your office? How 'bout putting it in the hallway?

- Go through drawers. You just might find a year's worth of sticky notes or enough pencils to supply a small school! Group all your postage stamps, paper clips, highlighter pens, and rubber bands together and put them where they belong. It's time to take control of your stuff and make things ordered.

- Take one last look around for clutter, and take it away.

Now that you can breathe, make an inventory of what you've got left:

- Do you have enough shelf space? Shelves will do more to keep your space neat than almost anything.

QUICK ⬤ PAINLESS

Here's a good rule of thumb: If the library or someone else has it, throw it out. You don't need your own copy of everything.

When it comes time to revamp your office, don't just rush out and buy stuff willy-nilly! Give yourself a week working in your office as-is—but write down everything that makes you say "if only I had...."

- Do you need more workspace—another table top on which to work?

- Do you have room for an extension of your desk or a table behind your desk? L-shaped and U-shaped configurations are efficient because you can often reach most important things with just a swivel of your chair.

- Try a shelf, within arm's reach, just above your desk. If you can reach it easily, it can hold all the stuff that normally collects on the desktop—stapler, tape, and clock, for example. This shelf is also an excellent place to store your most-used binders and the telephone book.

- Critically look at all your furniture; does it have a function? Would another file cabinet serve you better than a big bulky credenza? Would a bookcase be more useful than the small table that just collects magazines?

- Get a chair mat—especially if you're sitting on a carpeted surface—so you can swivel around your work area.

- Purchase a *big* wastepaper basket.

- Buy the best chair you can afford; if you spend more than a few hours a day in it, a well-designed, high-quality adjustable model is worth the investment. Let your visitors have the cheap chairs; you don't have time for an extended interruption anyway!

Regardless of how much time you spend at the office, anything you do to make it cheery and attractive will set a positive mood and increase your productivity. Here are a few suggestions for cosmetic touches:

- Are the walls clean and painted and light? A coat of paint can work inexpensive wonders for a dreary space.

- Make sure the windows get washed regularly.

- Hang curtains, drapes, or attractive shades.

- Put your awards and photographs in attractive frames.

- Hang framed art; it can be anything from a Picasso print to a Prince poster.

- Get a desk lamp (for task lighting) that you like. It needn't be an official office lamp; you can use anything meant for a living room or bedroom that sheds enough good light on your desk.

- If you have harsh overhead lighting, either change to softer light bulbs or purchase a floor lamp that meets your lighting needs while shedding a softer, more comfortable light.

- An area rug can add color and visual interest to your office.

- Stash small stuff in attractive baskets.

- Get yourself new desk accessories. Maybe a matching desk pad, pencil container, and memo pad holder would add a refined touch to your work environment. But remember, only get items that you will use, otherwise all you've done is added more clutter!

- Load magazines and journals that you must keep into magazine butlers—good looking ones—or place them on your shelves.

Congratulations! You are a master at getting things out of your space. You have so much room left now that you can fit in a great plant to fill an empty corner, to add softness, and to clean the air.

The Lazy Way

THE IDEAL DESK

If you've cleared off your desk at this point, you can, with care, put some things back. But remember that your desk is not a storage or warehousing facility for paper; it is a *work* area. Keep it clear, and you'll get more work done.

Everyday items such as a tape dispenser, stapler, pens and pencils, clock, and lamp can go back on your desk—if you don't have a nearby shelf or drawer to house them. Then, add your desktop files, described in the next section.

I'm going to walk you through a system that most of my clients have used with great success to keep their desks clear, to enable them to find papers again, and to quickly handle almost all of the mail that arrives in their offices.

The Desktop Filing System

This system works great to handle most of the mail that descends on you every day by giving you a place to quickly and easily house it. Get yourself some Eldon Add-A-Files; they have interlocking plastic pieces that, when joined together, make a holder for file folders in an upright position. You can also find these stands in metal—which is sturdier, of course—but they don't come in pieces, so you can't customize the size.

Place your file holder on a corner of your desk. Start with four pieces snapped together and see if you can't fit most of the files you need in a setup that deep. Because they're held in folders that are upright, you can easily see them and avoid the stacking syndrome. Many people swear that they always know what's in their stacks and

that's fine, but if you're having trouble finding things, it's time to get those folders standing at attention! Be sure the folders are labeled clearly and boldly. (I don't think typewritten labels are nearly big enough.)

Here's what folders might go into your desktop system:

- Bills to pay.

- To be filed.

- Take home.

- To assistant.

- To anyone else you routinely discuss things with; keep all the information in "their" folder, and you won't be looking for papers before your next meeting.

- Project I—the working folder of your most active project.

- Project II—same as Project I.

- Company I.

- Company II.

- Client Smith.

- Client Adams.

- To be copied.

- Cash receipts.

- Expense report.

Obviously, you aren't going to have all these files on your desktop, and you will have others specific to your situation. The idea is to have a place for your most frequently used files—maybe around 10 of them—so that as

If you'd like even more desktop space, get a movable arm and platform that lifts your computer monitor above the desk. It will bring the monitor into your line of vision and leave the area under it free.

paper comes in, you have a place to deposit it immediately.

As you finish Project A, you can remove its folder from the desktop and store it in a file cabinet. If your folders get too full, make another one, and mark it, for example, "Expense Reports II." Then, file Expense Reports I in the filing cabinet.

Some of you might claim that you can't find anything if papers are deposited into folders and aren't visible out on the desk. My response is that if you're reading this book, you probably need help organizing and that you can't find things with your present system any better. It might be true that some of your personal practices still aren't answering your needs any more than others' practices. I beg you, just try the desktop filing system (and anything else that appeals to you in this book) and see if you don't find some improvement.

So you have the everyday things parked in the best real estate zone—your desktop. The next most important level of paper should also end up close to you—ideally in a file drawer that's part of your desk. If you have a file cabinet within reach, that's another spot for files you need to access regularly.

MAKING THE MOST OF THE TIME YOU HAVE

Now that you've got your physical environment in shape, what do you do in your office so you can reclaim minutes and hours and days? Follow along. Adopt or adapt the following suggestions so that they're appropriate for you and your work situation.

The Mail

Ugh! So much paper flowing into your life, most of it brought by your friendly neighborhood mail carrier. Where does it all come from? The paperless society seems to be further from our reality as we stare at today's foot-high stack of incoming mail. Here are some coping mechanisms:

- Deal with your mail every day.

- As with the telephone, you want to stay in control. Don't let the sight of the mailman or mail cart be a signal for you to automatically drop everything and deal with the mail. You might be working on something more important, and it might be a better use of your time to go through the mail during a slower part of your day.

- If you have someone who could screen it and sort it before it gets to you, then by all means, assign that task to someone else!

- Throw out any junk mail without even opening it.

- Whenever possible, set aside time for mail handling so that you can immediately forward mail to others; jot a note at the bottom of something and send it on, or file what can be filed. That way, your mail will be more or less "finished" every day.

- Handle mail as few times as possible. For example, if you get a memo announcing a meeting, immediately pull out your calendar and jot down the time and date, and then toss the announcement. The wrong way to handle this is to read the announcement and

QUICK  PAINLESS

Keep a wastebasket right by the front door for immediate disposal of junk mail. It'll never have a chance to clutter up your home!

When in doubt, throw it out!

then put it in a pile for later. You'll undoubtedly end up rummaging through your piles of paper to find the announcement later or run across it two weeks after the meeting has been held.

- Any time you receive something marked "revised," find the old version and toss it! Replace it immediately with the new version.

- Whatever you can file in your desktop filing system should be filed now—not later.

Finessing the Fax

If there ever was a time-saver, it is the fax machine. Here are some ways to use it wisely:

- Use the fax to transmit information, saving you conversation time or leaving messages that might or might not get garbled at their destination.

- A fax is often considered documentation "in writing," which frequently seems to be required.

- Fax a note to someone who will need to think about his response.

- Fax a request for information that will require some research.

- Fax confirmations of meetings and appointments.

- Use the broadcast fax feature of your fax machine to automatically and simultaneously communicate with a predetermined group of people—all your sales people, for example.

- Send your faxed documents directly from your computer modem, saving the steps of printing out and then manually faxing.

- Receive your faxes from your computer; you won't need hard copies of most of your faxes and you can print only those you need to handle.

- A fax makes it easy for you to communicate when it's convenient for you; you can fax most people after office hours and on weekends.

- Your message might get more attention if it's waiting for the recipient when he or she arrives first thing in the morning.

Between the Covers

I've seen more wasted paper rolling off fax machines in the form of cover sheets. A whole $8\frac{1}{2}$"×11" sheet of paper is more space than you need to communicate that it's you faxing, how to contact you, the recipient, and how many pages you are faxing. It also takes much more time than necessary.

Here are some quick and easy alternatives:

- Use a sticky note, found in office supply stores, designed as a fax header. It has spaces for all the information required and is a mere $1\frac{1}{2}$"×4."

- If you're faxing a letter on your letterhead, start with one line that reads something like: "Three Page Faxed Document to Mr. Smith." That's really all you need to add to the information that's already on your stationery.

QUICK ⬛ PAINLESS

Sometimes, quick informality works even in business situations. If you receive a letter suggesting, say, a 10 o'clock meeting on January 4 at your office, scribble an okay on the letter and fax it to the sender. Done!

- If you do need a cover sheet, make it half a page ($8\frac{1}{2}"\times5\frac{1}{2}"$).

- Remember that cover sheets with logos and a lot of print add to transmission time and thus telephone costs; make your cover sheets clean and simple.

Note that you probably have to manually send a fax to someone who has a fax machine that instructs you to push the start key to begin transmission, but double check your manual if you have computer faxing software. Most have a keyboard command that will let you deal with such a situation.

The Wonders of Email

Yet another new development demanding your attention, email can be used efficiently to streamline communication. Email enables us to send written communication much faster than with a telephone call. Like all systems, you'll need a routine to handle email. Here's what works:

- Batch your work; in other words, collect and send email just a couple of times a day (or with the least frequency possible to enable you to keep up).

- Dump the jokes and trash or file for later reading.

- Scan your messages to see which ones can be answered with a couple of sentences. Answer them immediately.

- Then, handle the rest.

- Delete, delete, delete.

QUICK PAINLESS

Spend the time to preprogram the numbers in your fax machine or computer fax software that you fax frequently. This will save you hours in the long run.

- Organize an email filing system on your computer for those messages you must keep.
- Print hard copies of email messages as seldom as possible.
- If you have a feature that beeps you every time you receive an email message, do yourself a favor; reduce your stress and turn it off. Continual beeping is distracting; it might get you off focus and it could tempt you to interrupt yourself to see what's arrived.

THE SPIRAL NOTEBOOK SYSTEM

I've found that a small spiral notebook on my desk has been helpful as a "catch-all" for quick notes and various and sundry information I don't know where else to store.

My little notebook also acts as a telephone log; as I retrieve my voice-mail messages, I jot all the information into it. It's really come in handy; I've had reason to look back a few months for obscure numbers or names, and I always eventually find them in my notebook. I've noticed that I have fewer sticky notes around because everything goes into my little book.

THE TRUSTY TELEPHONE

The telephone has been with us a long time, relatively speaking, but it's surprising how many people have not yet learned how to manage it. It's so easy to let it control them rather than the other way around. The telephone is meant to serve you—not the other way around. If

YOU'LL THANK YOURSELF LATER

Be conscious of how much time you spend chit-chatting at the beginning and ending of your phone calls. Just making yourself aware of your pattern might help you to curb the time spent at the "ends" of your calls.

If you spend more than a couple of hours on the telephone every day, get yourself a telephone headset. They are relatively inexpensive and easy to use. Your hands stay free to type or file while you're chatting, and you'll feel the difference in your neck and shoulders at the end of the day.

you're feeling enslaved, you must get disciplined and tame the telephone into submission. Here's how:

- Don't pick it up. If you're in the middle of something or in deep concentration, let the answering machine, voice mail, or your assistant handle it.

- Consider getting caller ID. The newer models will display not just the number, but also the name of the person calling you. If you've got a busy day ahead of you, that little box could save you countless minutes of fending off telemarketers and that well-meaning friend or relative who never gets the hint to cut the call short.

- If you have to, turn off the ringer.

- Retrieve your messages a few times a day.

- Schedule specific times at which you make a batch of return calls.

- Program all your speed-dial telephone numbers.

- Use your voice-mail features, if you have them, to send the same message to a specific group of people at the push of a button.

- Your outgoing message should make it clear when the caller might expect to hear back from you.

- I always leave my fax number on my outgoing message and encourage callers to use it if appropriate.

- Ask your callers to state their purpose or ask their question so that you can get back to them well prepared.

Leave good messages. There's nothing more frustrating than listening to rapid-fire messages from someone I don't know, requiring me to replay their message several times to get all the information.

Speak slowly and clearly; you know what your name is, but the person listening to the message might not, and if you say it in one rushed sound bite, he still won't know. State your telephone number at the beginning *and* the end of your message, and let the person you're calling know a good time to get back to you.

Another way to most effectively use the telephone—if you're doing the calling—is to be sure you stay on track during your conversation. Notes that you've jotted down—a quick form of agenda—will help you get to the point and stay there during a telephone conversation.

MEETINGS

Sometimes the biggest time-wasters in a person's day, meetings can cause endless frustration. Within the parameters of your authority, consider these suggestions:

- Determine whether the meeting is really necessary. Just because you've always had team meetings every Friday morning since the company was founded doesn't mean that they're necessary. Rethink old habits.

- Can you accomplish the same work another way? If you're just disseminating information, perhaps you could simply send email to everyone involved. A conference call might do the job as well or better.

QUICK ⬤ PAINLESS

If you have a telephone with a speaker, use it while you're on hold. You'll be free to roam around while you're waiting, and you will hear through the speaker when the person gets back on the line.

- Does everyone at the meeting need to be there? Don't involve any more people than absolutely necessary. Remember that a one-hour meeting with five attendees is five work hours!

- Opt for a meeting if you need face-to-face input, group interaction, or reaching agreement. Be sure your meetings have a clear objective.

- Does every meeting have an agenda? An agenda will indicate to everyone involved that "This is the plan, and you've got to work the plan."

- Start on time; don't wait for late-comers.

- Announce the time the meeting will end and end on time.

- Be sure that you're prepared and that you have all your materials in place.

- If you're in charge, check with other participants beforehand. Confirm their responsibilities and the length of time you've allotted to them.

- Always set up the next meeting while everyone is present and you'll save yourself or someone else many minutes of trying to coordinate everyone's schedules later. This is also why it's a good idea to take your planner with you everywhere you go.

- If assignments are delegated during the meeting, be clear about the job and the due date.

YOU'LL THANK YOURSELF LATER

Rethink your participation at meetings. If there's no specific reason for you to be there—and if you have a choice—make a phone call and graciously excuse yourself. Get something done instead.

Getting Time on Your Side

	The Old Way	The Lazy Way
Faxing a letter	10 minutes (printing it and manually sending it)	1 minute (direct from the computer). Look, Ma—no paper!
Handling your mail	40 percent handled in 30 minutes; the rest is here somewhere…	90 percent handled in 10 minutes
A 20-minute meeting	50 minutes	15 minutes
Average number of telephone interruptions per day	13	3 (you turned off the ringer)
Finding the material you wanted to go over with Bob at your weekly meeting	9 minutes (most of the things you needed)	9 seconds (it's all in the desktop folder marked "Bob")
How many magazines you have in your office to be read	23	2 magazines and 45 pages of articles in a "To Read" folder

Chapter

ten

Time-Savers at Home

Home: Is it a respite in a frantic world or just another frantic world in itself? If you've got a spouse, kids, pets, automobiles, house, friends, volunteer work, and social life, you probably have a bit of a circus when you walk in the door. Because you're reading this book, I guess that you're interested in some of the following issues:

- A calmer, less confused home life
- The ability to find things when you need them
- Not spending all your free time working on house projects
- Minimizing the amount of time and energy you spend in the kitchen
- Maximizing the amount of time you spend with your spouse and children
- Not having so much "stuff" to deal with
- Having a clean, attractive, uncluttered home environment

Read on for techniques that will help you minimize confusion and establish some systems that will make home life positively pleasurable. The most important thing to remember is that organization is the key to a smooth-running household.

First, I walk you through your belongings so you can eliminate what you don't use—a great first step with enormous impact. Then, I give you some suggestions about how to organize what you have left so you can find your belongings and use them. Lastly, I discuss how to maximize your personal time so that you can spend as much time as possible with the people you love.

SIMPLIFY

The Lazy Way home is a simple home—or at least a simpler place. Simplification comes about through some soul-searching and some action steps.

Take some time to think about how you and your family can simplify your life together. Have you been on the super-fast track to success? Caught up in acquiring the trappings success brings? Overloaded with stuff? Does it seem you rarely have the time to enjoy them?

The corporate rat race might be just what brings you joy, but when did you last sit down and think about it? Have you stopped long enough to consider where you're going and what makes you happy? If you're having trouble meeting the needs of your work and your family, maybe it's time for a timeout to think about your priorities.

Simplifying Stuff

The ability to buy a lot of things might have gotten you a lot of stuff without enhancing your life in any

YOU'LL THANK YOURSELF LATER

Put all rosters—the Little League team, the Garden Club membership, and the homeowners' association for example—in a binder by the telephone. Three-hole-punch new rosters as they arrive and replace the outdated ones.

measurable way. In fact, all that stuff could be a big reason for your lack of time and overabundance of stress.

The fact is that everything you own needs to be maintained, repaired, stored, insured, or upgraded. Each one of those activities requires time. Re-think your priorities as they relate to what you own. Is owning a Harley, an RV, and a snowmobile enriching your life or just putting more demands on it? Do your computers, printers, and electronic organizers help you or add to your lists of maintenance projects? Do you have closets full of clothes that you rarely wear?

Think seriously about cutting back. Remember that someone else needs and can use your stuff. Which of all your belongings can you weed out? And how? For super tips, read the Cox/Evatt book, *30 Days to a Simpler Life*. In the meantime, here are some suggestions about what to do with your purged belongings. Then, I go through your house room-by-room and organize what you have left:

- **Sell them.** At least you'll get some cash back in addition to the space you'll reclaim.

- **Recycle.** Try not to add to the landfill problem.

- **Consign.** Let someone else sell your belongings; you'll get some return on your dollar and be content with the thought that someone got what he needed.

- **Thrift shop.** Support your local charity or church and those in need by donating your belongings to their thrift shop. Don't forget to keep your receipt so you'll get a tax deduction.

QUICK ⬤ PAINLESS

We live in such an affluent society that we're burdened by belongings we don't even buy or want. Don't accept an offering just because it's free. There is a price for everything!

■ **Hospitals and nursing homes.** These places often welcome discards such as books, magazines, and video tapes. Be sure to call first to determine whether they need these items.

■ **The Salvation Army.** Not only will they take almost anything you have to offer, but they will also pick up your donations, leave you a receipt for tax purposes, and put people to work.

■ **Toss.** Sometimes, it's just not worth the effort to find the right recipient for an irreparably broken, stained, or out-of-date item. Let it go.

Here are important areas where you can benefit from organizing. Take a project or room one at a time. Enjoy the process, and know that your life will become easier every step you take:

■ Books—Make a clean sweep of every bookshelf. If you've got a bookstore nearby that buys and sells used books, take them there. Involve your children in this; ask them where they'd like to see their old books go.

■ Kitchen—Sort through every cupboard and shelf, taking out anything you haven't used in a year (or 10). Place these things in the thrift shop or Salvation Army heap. Then, go through remaining dishes and glassware, eliminating anything that is stained, chipped, cracked, or just plain broken. Toss these out! Keep only the kitchen appliances you use regularly. You can probably let the electric paring knives and melon-ballers go.

■ Paper—Paper is absolutely, without a doubt, the number one source of my clients' frustrations. It overwhelms all of us. We're going to set up an office space for you later in this chapter, but first, you must get rid of every scrap of paper you can.

Basically, you should keep anything related to a tax return because these items could be proof of a legitimate expense should the IRS audit you. Sentimental stuff can be saved—within reason. I get to that later. Feel free to toss coupons, grocery receipts, charge slips for anything not deductible, utility bills, monthly charge card statements, and monthly investment statements—but keep the year-end statements.

Let go of magazines, newsletters, and catalogs. Remember that it's the library's job to store reading materials.

If you run across several years worth of tax returns—and related documentation such as bank statements, canceled checks, and receipts—and papers related to real-estate purchases and sales, pack them up into banker's boxes and store them out of the way. You should probably keep property information forever; keep tax information for seven years to be on the safe side. Otherwise, take your accountant's advice.

■ Closets—Get rid of everything you haven't worn in a year or two. Eliminate your skinny clothes and your fat clothes. Inventory every drawer and edit, edit, edit. Keep the best; leave the rest.

Congratulations! It took a lot of strength and willpower to get rid of all those clothes you feel attached to. Reward yourself with that beautiful shirt you've been coveting.

The Lazy Way

Organization is not a one-shot deal. After you have set up systems that work for you in your home, only daily, weekly, and monthly maintenance will keep you organized.

- Electronics—How many boom boxes do you actually need? When did you last view those video movies you own? Just how long are you going to hang on to your LPs? When was the last time the kids played with their Game Boys? Be strong. Clear 'em out. (Not the kids—the Game Boys!)

- Linen closets—Make it a rule that you will only own matching sheet sets, good towels, and one extra blanket per bed. Orphan sheets, pillow cases, and anything that looks like stringy terry cloth goes—not to mention those 11 extra blankets.

- Toys—Admit it! Your kids probably don't play with two thirds of the toys that they have accumulated—and that you consistently trip over. Enlist their help in purging, and at the same time, teach them that sharing with others less fortunate is an honorable venture. Put a third of whatever's left away and out of sight. Pull this supply of toys out on the next rainy day or home-from-school day to enliven their play when they start to get bored.

- The garage—Ugh. Most everyone's garage is pretty overwhelming, but if you break down the chore into a few hours a week for several weeks, you will make great progress, I promise. If you're tired of running the car into luggage you haven't used for 10 years and looking at a lawn mower that doesn't work and old dried-up cans of paint, you will feel so much better when these things have disappeared. Later, you can organize what's left.

You've Purged; Now Merge

Now that you've eliminated duplicates, too small, too many, wrong color, missing pieces, broken, worn out, faded, warped, scratched, old, too large, smashed, and other doubtful contributors to your quality of life, you can go on to the next step: organizing what you have left. Good organization is the quickest way to good time management. (See my book *Organize Your Stuff the Lazy Way* for a more thorough discussion of how to organize every room in the house.)

Organization is going to save you time because:

- You won't have to spend time searching the house from top to bottom for things any more because you know where everything is.

- You won't come home from the store with something just to realize that you already have one.

- You won't spend time washing things that don't need washing.

- You will spend less time cleaning.

- You will pay your bills on time.

- You will make fewer trips to the post office, dry cleaners, grocery store, video store, library, and school.

Sound heavenly? Well, you won't exactly reach Nirvana with good organization, but all of this will help you keep your life moving smoothly, like a well-oiled machine. Here are some ways to get your abode organized so that you can start on the path towards bliss— *The Lazy Way*.

QUICK ◗▩◖ PAINLESS

KEEPING THE KITCHEN CONTROLLED

Because it's the heart of the house for most families, the kitchen takes a beating. Pare it down to the bare essentials to keep it in top condition. Assuming you've cleared out everything that could go away, start by cleaning out drawers, cupboards, and shelves:

- Line everything with bright shelf paper before putting your belongings back.

- Use baskets to hold small stuff such as soup mixes and sauce envelopes.

- Put your spice jars on lazy Susans for easy retrieval. (I bet you'll find some spices from your grandmother's kitchen you can toss.)

- Gather things that get used together and put them away together. Coffee fixings, stuff for making sack lunches, and baking supplies are good examples.

- Clear the counters of everything except for those items you need every single day. You don't need a set of canisters on the counter top with flour and sugar handy if you rarely use flour and sugar.

- Install hooks to keep the most-used items handy. For example, you might want to hang your dish brush, hot pads, and dish towels within easy reach.

- Store special china and serving pieces in the dining room or pantry if you have one.

- Add shelves to tall cupboards if you don't need the height. You'll double your storage room.

Congratulations! You've got your meal lists written down, and that made your shopping trip much easier. Now, sit down with your feet up and enjoy a glass of wine and some of that lovely cheese you brought home.

The Lazy Way

- Put your vitamins and supplements together in a basket and get them off the counter into a handy cupboard.

- If you've got a first-generation microwave that's about the size of a New York City apartment, consider replacing it with a newer, streamlined one. It will take much less space. The same thing applies to can openers, toaster ovens, and other appliances.

- Install cup hooks in the top of a cupboard to save space.

- Put stemware tracks in the top of a cupboard. The base of stemmed glassware slides between two tracks, storing the glass upside down and dust free.

- If you have pretty pots and pans and some hanging room, install a wrought-iron pot rack against a wall or over the stove for a dramatic touch.

- Store your bottles of oil and vinegar on a pretty tray in a cupboard. Clean up will be easy.

- Clear the refrigerator of all the magnets and pieces of paper. I offer suggestions about what to do with family information later in this chapter.

Now that you've got the heart of the house under control, it's time to take the biggest step you can to manage your time well at home. It's all about setting up an office—if you don't already have one in place.

YOUR OFFICE

Essential to running a household smoothly—and having a place to house paper—is a designated work area. The

Designate an attractive basket to hold all your to-be-read materials. When it gets full, pull the stuff from the bottom and convince yourself to toss it.

absolute minimum requirements are a desk (or work surface of some kind), a file cabinet, and a nearby telephone. You'll also need shelves or bookcases to hold supplies, books, and binders. Computers, fax machines, copiers, and other assorted equipment are great—but only if you need them and can afford them. See Chapter 2, "Bringing in the Heavy Hitters," for a list of office equipment and how to use it.

Fast Filing

After setting up a workspace, the next crucial step is to establish a filing system. A filing cabinet will give you a place for everything that comes your way and that you need to keep. Here's the basic outline and suggestions for files:

- Bills to pay.
- To be filed.
- Medical info—Just one, or one per family member.
- Medical bills.
- Insurance—One folder per kind of insurance.
- Mortgage.
- Bank statements—Take them out of their envelopes and unfold them. Store canceled checks in boxes.
- Credit cards—One per card.
- Utilities—Probably all together in one folder. You most likely don't need to keep more than the last month's bill.
- Investments—One folder per account.

- Instructions and warranties.

- Auto.

- Property taxes.

- Current year taxes—To collect items that don't belong in other categories.

- Past taxes—You might find it handy to keep one or two years' back tax returns handy.

- Each child—Deposit medical records or report cards or drawings or whatever you want to keep for awhile.

- Charitable receipts—If you've only got a few, skip this folder and put the receipts into current year's tax folder.

- Pets.

Obviously, this list is generic; you will undoubtedly have additions and deletions according to your family's individual needs.

Step two of the filing process is less business-like and more personal. This is where you'll make folders for the fun stuff in your life:

- Articles to read—From magazines and newspapers.

- Travel.

- House and garden ideas.

- Organizations—A folder for each.

- Correspondence to answer.

- Correspondence to save.

- Any hobbies—Like your horse-breeding information or stamp-collecting pamphlets.

QUICK PAINLESS

Remember: A filing system is only good if you use it! Force yourself to file at least once a week so you don't get behind.

Make a folder for anyone to whom you regularly pass on information. For example, a file for your spouse might be handy so the things he or she has to see is all together in one place and not lying all over your desk. If you regularly send pictures to Grandma, make a folder for her. I cut out funny or interesting articles (at least I think they're funny and interesting) for my kids and collect them in a folder. When I've got an envelope's worth, I send it.

Painless Paperwork

During my career as a professional organizer, I have seen nothing that causes people more pain than paper. We are all overwhelmed by it, and controlling it seems a futile battle. But all is not lost. There are ways to minimize the amount of paper that comes into our lives, and if you've set up an office and filing system as described earlier in this chapter, here's where you learn how to use that system.

Cut It Off at the Pass

The best trick for cutting down on paper is not to let it get into your house in the first place. Here's how:

- Do your first sort and toss junk mail—unopened— next to your mail box, the mail slot, or while you're still at the post office to pick it up. There's absolutely no reason for you to keep subscription offers, charitable solicitations, catalogs, credit card applications, and the like if you know you aren't interested. Banish them immediately!

Congratulations! You've made all your folders and filed away your papers. Treat yourself to a beautiful plant that you can place where papers used to be stacked.

The Lazy Way

- Spend the time to mail in labels from catalogs and ask to be taken off their mailing lists.

- If you get duplicate issues of a catalog you enjoy receiving, send the company the duplicate label and ask it to delete that listing.

You should have considerably less mail after tossing the junk. Here's what you do with what's left. The secret to managing paper is to keep on top of it—to deal with it every day so that you don't get behind. You might have heard the advice to "handle paper only once." I don't think that's quite realistic, but you do want to attempt to handle it as few times as possible:

- If you're like most folks, you'll have bills to pay. Deposit them immediately into the Bills to Pay folder. If you pay bills twice a month—and you shouldn't do it more frequently than that—make up two folders. On the outside of one folder, list the names of creditors whom you pay around the first of every month; the second folder should list and hold the bills you pay around the 15th. Virtually all bills go into one of these two folders and only come out again when you pay them.

- You might receive mail that simply needs to be filed without any action; an investment account statement is a good example. File that mail immediately.

- Magazines and periodicals—flip through questionable ones and toss them out (recycle, please) if they don't grab you. The rest go into your reading basket.

QUICK ⚫ PAINLESS

If there's room, place a large wastebasket right by the mail's point of entry so there's no chance the junk can get any further in the house.

- Then, you might have something your spouse needs to see before filing or that you'd like to discuss with your child; file it in the appropriate person's folder.

- Got something you'd like to work on at the office? Put it in your briefcase or tote immediately.

Waging War on Junk Mail

Take action to remove yourself from all mailing lists and discourage your being added to new lists. Write to

Direct Marketing Association
P.O. Box 9008
Farmingdale, NY 11735-9008

Ask that they remove you from their mailing lists and forbid them to sell or rent your name and address. This will help. For the most significant impact on the amount of paper showing up at your door, remember to

- Give them all the variations of your name: Betty Smith, Betty J. Smith, Mrs. Robert Smith, B. J. Smith.

- Your name will be hot property again as soon as you order something with a credit card. This means you'll have to repeat this process at least a couple of times a year.

- The easiest way to make these requests is to have a supply of one form letter that you can pop into an envelope regularly.

Family Information

LifeLinks products (manufactured by At-A-Glance) offers a "Family Central" binder with preprinted forms and

Good going! You've sent a letter requesting to be removed from mailing lists and you should see results in a month or so. In the meantime, make yourself a cup of tea and read your novel for half an hour.

The Lazy Way

tabs to track family members' health records, the family pet record, bank and credit records, budgeting forms, and a month-by-month home maintenance guide—just to name a few. If you do only one thing as a result of reading this book, it should be to fill out and use the Family Central binder.

The Perfect Pending Folder

A place for short-term pending issues is a solution many of my clients could not do without. Into your pending folder might go letters to which you are waiting a response, invitations, tickets to upcoming events, pending health insurance claims, and the page torn from a catalog that has your order number and date written on it. Be sure to note future dates and times in your date book before filing. Anything that is not quite completed, that doesn't require its own file, and that would otherwise float around on the top of your desk for weeks goes into the pending folder.

CLOTHES, CLOSETS, AND CONTROL

Once again, we're victims of our affluence. Our stuff magically multiplies, and nothing except paper multiplies as fast as clothing in most homes.

Here are some quick and easy ways to regain control of your closets:

- Pull out of the closets all clothing that needs repair, mending, buttons, alterations, cleaning, or ironing. Put the appropriate ones in the car so they're sure to get to their destination.

IF YOU'RE SO INCLINED

If repeated requests to a company or organization haven't worked to get you off their mailing list, try this method: Stuff their postage-paid envelope with the solicitation they sent to you and as much other discarded mail as will fit. Include another request to be removed from the list, and sign and date it. Seal it up, and send it back to the company. This technique will cost them money and get their attention!

- If you have a huge saved-up stack of mending or ironing—or both!—hire someone to take care of the lot in one fell swoop. Then, you can keep up instead of catch up.

- If you have clothing you know a friend or relative could use, pack it up—now—and get it to the post office.

- Rehang suits or matching tops and bottoms on suit hangers (you know, the ones that hold both a top and bottom).

- Add a second hanging bar if you have more "short" items—such as shirts and blouses—than long ones.

- Maximize the space above existing shelves in closets: there's usually room for an additional shelf. Use the new shelf for out of season clothes.

- Pack accessories in see-through plastic bins.

- Store shoes in hanging bags, a shoe caddy, plastic boxes, or special shoe cupboards.

- If your closet space is tight, store ski clothes or other sports equipment, ball gowns, and your off-season wardrobe elsewhere.

- Store off-season shoes or sweaters or bikinis in plastic bins meant for holding gift wrap. Shove them under the bed.

- Install hooks wherever you can—inside the closets, by the shower, and behind doors.

- If you're organizing kids, put hooks and closet rods at their height.

YOU'LL THANK YOURSELF LATER

Obviously, life happens: Emergencies pop up, plans change, and forces of nature conspire to challenge the best-laid plans. The best you can do is stay flexible and put your sense of humor to work.

- The coat closet might accommodate more shelves with open bins in them to collect mittens, scarves, and hats. Have I said this already? Add sturdy hooks!

- Don't forget to look at Chapter 5, "Follow Up and Follow Through," for resources to help.

MAKING QUICK WORK OF COOKING

If time is at a premium for you, you might find that meal preparation is something you'd love to banish. If only we all didn't need food so often! You can take some short-cuts to simplify the business of stayin' alive.

First of all, you might be overly ambitious in your desire to do a great job in the kitchen. Try lowering your standards and prepare healthy, hearty but maintenance-style food during the week. Be creative and spend more time on the weekends if that's what floats your boat.

Here's a system you might want to try:

- Create a list of 12 main dishes—the guaranteed tried-and-true winners—at your house. With dinners out and leftovers, these 12 dishes should see you through three whole weeks.

- Then, write down a second list of all the starches and vegetables and side dishes your family likes.

- Take these two lists with you to the grocery store. You won't have to be creative on your feet because all your ideas are on your lists. Pull a few things from the main dish list and a few from the side dish list, and you've got several dinners in your cart.

- You'll probably add to your cart fruits, staples, breakfast foods, and sweets for variety.

QUICK ⬤ PAINLESS

In case no one's ever told you to hang up your clothes and put them away as soon as you take them off, allow me. Nothing will do more to keep you organized in the bedroom and bathroom than putting your clothes back in closets or in the laundry.

Use the following list for some more time-saving ideas. Check out Chapter 4, for suggestions on how to delegate kitchen responsibilities.

- Cook large batches of things that can be made in quantity—lasagna, stews, and soups, for example—and freeze for the future.

- A roasted chicken should suffice for two dinners.

- At least on weekdays, eliminate serving platters by serving portions directly from the stove.

- Make enough so that you end up with leftovers that can go into sack lunches the next day.

- There's no rule that you have to have meat and potatoes for dinner. Try a pot of oatmeal, pancakes, or French toast, all with fresh fruit. Really, it's allowed!

- Line roasting pans with heavy-duty aluminum foil, and clean-up will be a breeze.

- Buy some things in bulk. Canned tomatoes, ground beef, ketchup and mustards, pasta, refried beans, and soups are all good to have on hand; you'll always be able to whip up a meal.

- Clean up kitchen spills when they happen; dried-on goop is much harder to clean and will take more time.

- Grab a handful of exotic mixed greens from the salad bar to add to your plain green salad.

- Order a nice entree from a local restaurant or deli and pick it up on the way home from work. Add rice

IF YOU'RE SO
INCLINED

Do you have a child who's showing some interest in cooking? Spend some time showing him or her how to roast a chicken, assemble burritos, or start a soup pot brewing.

or potatoes and a green vegetable, and dinner's ready in no time!

■ If you still have it, pull out the cookbook that came with your microwave and learn some new time-saving techniques from it.

■ When all else fails, eat a big lunch—and have a yogurt for dinner!

QUICK ▬ PAINLESS

For the last word on easy cooking, read *Cook Your Meals the Lazy Way*, by Sharon Bowers. It offers a wealth of wonderful ideas and shows you how to "go from pot to plate without breaking a sweat."

Getting Time on Your Side

	The Old Way	The Lazy Way
Opening and reading your mail	35 minutes	3 minutes (ignoring the junk mail)
Getting dinner on the table	80 minutes	35 minutes
Finding the telephone number of the Girl Scout leader	15 minutes and 2 telephone calls to ask around	1 minute; it's in the roster binder
Picking out an outfit for tomorrow	12 minutes	2 minutes
Finding last year's tax return	3 hours (over a week's time)	$1^{1}/_{2}$ minutes (in the file cabinet, silly!)
Paying bills	Just finding them all took an hour	1 hour

Fitting Family Life into the Puzzle

The fast pace of the lifestyle many of us lead today is making a significant impact on our personal lives. Do you often feel as though your family is getting shortchanged or feel frequent guilt because you're torn between your work and your family? Is your family making noises about not seeing enough of you—or even getting downright resentful about your absences? An alarm is sounding, and you'd better pay attention. Because you're reading this book, you're probably ready to make some changes.

Other chapters will give you many ideas on how to streamline your time on the job and make some household chores go faster. This chapter deals specifically with making time for your partner, spouse, or children—or anyone else you live with and want time for—as well as how to establish some systems to keep the lines of communication open and to simplify everyday life.

The phrase bears repeating: "No one ever wished on her death bed that she'd spent more time at the office." Let's see how you might spend more and better time at home. And then, when you get there, how do you keep things pleasant and somewhat under control?

TIME COMMITMENTS

If you've taken on more than you can handle in your personal life, consider what can be eliminated. The more you've committed to, the less time you're going to have, and the more stress you undoubtedly will experience. There are ways to make a contribution to the world around you and causes that are important to you that still allow you to get to your first priorities first. Here are some questions to ask yourself:

- Are there any activities in your life that should be completely eliminated? Have you simply continued a pattern of involvement in something—just because it's a habit? It's time to stop for a few minutes and reconsider. You might find a couple of activities that should have been eliminated months— or years—ago!

- Can you share the duties required of an extracurricular activity with someone else? Avoid the temptation of being all things to all people. Let someone else take up the slack for a change. If you think you're the only one who can do the job, think again!

- Can you co-chair an event rather than be the only chairperson? This might take some self-discipline on your part to give up the control you may enjoy when you're in charge, but think about how else you could be spending your time if you relinquish the reins.

- Can you change your membership status in your organization from active to associate or inactive? You don't have to be the most productive volunteer that your organization's ever seen, you know!

- Can you cut back some function or chore from every week to every other week or from every month to every quarter?

- Can you work on a committee rather than chair the committee? You can still be very valuable and pro-ductive as a worker bee—maybe even more so—than as the administrator.

IF YOU CAN'T BEAT 'EM, JOIN 'EM

Besides completely extricating yourself from some out-side interests, think about what you can do with family members that allow you to pursue the interests you don't want to give up. See whether it's possible to join forces by involving two or more family members in the same activity. Perhaps your spouse would participate in your prayer group, turning it into a shared activity rather than another activity that takes you away from home. Conversely, you might choose to get involved in the activities of other family members. For example, if you're no longer rewarded by the time you're spending at your book club, graciously withdraw and sign up to coach

QUICK PAINLESS

Keep your loved ones at the top of your "to do" list and you'll feel a lot better about the time you inevitably have to spend away from them.

What better way to spend time together than exercising or enjoying a new sport? Perhaps you and your spouse could sign up for tennis lessons together. Why not take the whole family to try cross-country skiing if they're willing? Or take the kids to the club and work out with them. (Try to ignore the fact that they will learn faster and do better than you after the first 20 minutes!)

your child's soccer team. It's all about making conscious decisions and choices based on your priorities.

How else do you increase the hours you spend with family? If you've decided that "more family time" is near the top of your priority list, scheduling is the only way. Use your planner and make appointments to block out family time. The results might look like this:

- It might mean striking through every Wednesday afternoon to catch your son's softball game.
- It will undoubtedly mean getting away for a weekend—or at least overnight—with your spouse. Regularly.
- It might mean a monthly lunch date with your daughter.
- It will mean planning a vacation for the family.
- It might mean a once-a-week breakfast meeting with your sister.
- It might mean shipping the kids off to friends so you and your partner can be alone.
- Each parent might book a whole weekend day with each child. There's nothing like one-on-one!

Getting Everyone on the Same Page

Integrating everyone's schedules in a busy family can be a major feat. Every family is different, of course. You might have a baby with very few of her own plans. You might also have a house full of teenagers with after-school activities, sports events, and jobs. If you're closer to the second description, keep reading for helpful ideas to make all the pieces mesh.

Start at the beginning of every school year, and jot down the other family members' important dates in your planner. Make note of your children's vacations, holidays, meetings, and sporting events. As soon as bulletins come home from school, be sure that you mark new events and dates in your planner. You'll find it handy to have this information if you need to plan and the children aren't around.

Communications from school don't always make it home. When they do, they might not make it all the way to you. Train your kids to regularly empty their backpacks and pass on to you the notices and announcements you need to see. You'll probably also have to ask whether there are notices for parents or spend the time to physically go through your child's backpack with him or her.

The Family Calendar

The one exception to the one-calendar rule is the family calendar. What works best is a shared wall calendar hung on a kitchen wall or other centrally located spot. Here's where everyone (you hope) will jot down the activities that will impact others in the family, such as sports events, school plays, doctor's and dentist's appointments, and family outings. It will provide an overview of who is where, who is busy, what's coming up, and a way to get in touch with family members in case they're needed.

A handy tool to increase communication at home is Day Runner's Home Manager Organizer. This product

IF YOU'RE SO
INCLINED

I always made a copy of my kids' daily schedule at school and kept it with me in my planner. That way, when I had to make appointments for them during the school day, I could often schedule times when they were in P.E. or study hall. (Warning: They'll be bummed that they aren't missing math or history class if you use this system!)

If your kids are having a hard time remembering how to take complete messages, try putting it into a context that works for them. After all, they'd be pretty upset if they missed a play-date because someone didn't get all the info, right?

attaches to the refrigerator door or wall and replaces a myriad of messy notes, schedules, messages, lists, and the like. It's got a monthly calendar, a pen and pencil holder, a place for sticky notes, and a dry-erase board on which to write messages. The calendar is large enough to jot down a few entries per day; if it's put in a visible place (and used regularly), it will vastly improve intra-family communication.

On the subject of messages, take the time to train your children—sooner, rather than later—to take proper messages. Explain that just as they want to know who called for them and how to get in touch with the caller, you need the same consideration. If you have a message pad (preferably with carbon paper underneath so there's always a copy left), it might prompt them to also fill out the date, time, and whether you're required to call back. Getting the message right the first time will save you a lot of time trying to figure out who called or why.

Not only does your personal information go on the family calendar, but also the reverse is true: You need to make note in your personal planner of family members' important entries as they come up. You might not need to remember your daughter's dentist appointment, but you will want to block out the evening she's performing in the school play. It takes training to learn how to do all of it correctly.

Nights at the Round Table

Face-to-face communication between all family members is another good way to coordinate schedules. You can call a Sunday evening meeting and go over schedules then. Or you might prefer to start with a session with your spouse and integrate activities for the two of you. Then, wander from child to child to check on their plans for the coming week.

Family meetings are also a good time to discuss vacations or how to spend Christmas. (Obviously, small children will not have a clue about their agendas; coordinating is meant for older children.) Even if you don't have pressing issues every week, get together anyway. Regularly scheduled family gatherings can be a good opportunity for busy adults and kids to connect with each other. You might also make a bit of an event of it; what if you were to make it "hot fudge sundae" night as well as meeting night?

HELPING KIDS HELP THEMSELVES

You will grant your children a huge gift, and help them get a step ahead of the crowd, by teaching them how to manage their time. Kids' lives are often as complicated as their parents, and they need all the help they can get. As in your case, using a planner is one of the best techniques to help them sort out their lives.

Of course, any new habit requires a short-term investment of time for long-term time-savings. If your kids become somewhat organized and trained to think ahead (we can dream, can't we?), you just might avoid some last-minute crises, which are guaranteed to create havoc in your schedule.

Congratulations! You've started your kids on the right track to being better organized. Celebrate by going out for ice cream.

I know all of this planning sounds like a deluded person's fantasy if you've got sullen or hostile teenagers at home who don't mind missing appointments, who aren't at *all* worried about their chores, and who certainly don't concern themselves with what's growing in their closet or under their bed. But approaching in the right spirit—without creating a power struggle—you might make some headway:

- How many times has your teen dashed in to say that he just remembered a practice session that starts in 10 minutes and could you please drive him?

- Has a child ever asked you to help her with a report that you hadn't heard about until now and that is due tomorrow?

- How many surprise volunteer jobs at school have your kids signed you up for?

- How did you like spending a Saturday night driving four kids to a rock concert when you'd planned a date with a mystery novel or had to finish a report for work?

The Power of the Spoken Word

Communication is the key. Sit those kids down and nicely explain the facts of life. You want nothing more than to help them, but you must know in advance—whenever possible—what they're going to need from you and when. Of course, this is not going to work all the time, and there will always be mix-ups. But communicating clearly is a great first step, and you will teach them respect for your time by respecting theirs.

Congratulations! You and your family have made it through a week without any last-minute rememberings! Take everyone out to the park for a picnic!

The Lazy Way

Taking a Grown-Up Step

Take those same children to the office supply store and buy them organizers. Day-Timers and Day Runner both make Student Planner systems with snappy-looking pages. Besides the one-week-on-two-pages calendar, there are a whole wardrobe of filler sheets to customize your student's planner. Among them are pages for class schedules, monthly planning sheets, class-assignment sheets, grade-tracking sheets, and address and phone directory pages. You can also add note pads and a selection of covers to hold the systems.

Learning the Ropes

The next step of teen time-management training is sitting down with them and helping them fill in their schedules:

- They'll note due dates for homework projects.
- They need to block out time for their jobs.
- They need to schedule their assigned household chores.
- They need help remembering important birthdays (yours!).
- They should write in the sports events they're slated to participate in or attend.
- They'll want to write in extracurricular activities.
- They need to note appointments with doctors, dentists, tutors, and the orthodontist.
- They'll want to block out all vacations and days off school.

QUICK PAINLESS

See what your child thinks of an "academic" planner; they start in September and end in August of the following year. It makes a lot of sense to me; when my kids were in school, I always thought of September as New Year's.

Schoolwork

My kids weren't alone, I suspect, when they said, "No, Mom, I don't need to write it down; I won't forget." They forgot a lot of times. Encourage them to take their planners to school with them and to write down their assignments, due dates, and the exact subject matter. (It's amazing how unclear teachers can be about homework assignments, isn't it?)

To really show them the value of their planners, take one of their projects and map it out as you would for yourself. Starting with the due date, show them how to work backwards and how to set interim deadlines for each step of their project.

TEACHING LESSON, SAVING TIME

In case your little darlings don't have chores, allow me to encourage you to change that. Kids—at an early age—need to participate in the business of family living. If they're tall enough to reach the table, they can set it or clear it. If they have the energy to play with their toys, they can manage to pick them up. You can teach young teens how to use the washing machine or at least collect dirty laundry and distribute clean laundry. Not only will you teach them valuable lessons about sharing the workload, being a team player, and responsibility, but also you won't spend all your time doing all the work!

The Job Grid

Discussing chores (or in the worst-case scenario, arguing about chores) can take a lot of time if you let it. You

QUICK ⬤ *PAINLESS*

One way to eke out a little more one-on-one time with a child is to do different things—but together. For example, catch up on your reading while your child does his homework in the same room. While your daughter's doing the dishes, make your grocery list or write a quick letter to a friend while sitting at the kitchen table.

might have fewer discussions with the help of a printed chart, written with input from your kids, where you note the jobs and who is to do them when. Somehow, a job sheet printed and tacked to the wall makes the plan seem a little more "official." It might cut down on the discussion time. It helped me when I had children at home, so it's certainly worth a try at your house.

Start with a grid, with chores listed along the top of the grid and your kids' names listed down the left side. Or make a chart for each child, with Monday through Sunday at the top and the chores listed down the left side. Whatever visually communicates what's to be done leaves one less thing for you to discuss.

Planning Chores

Get your older children to incorporate their chores into their planners as they would a doctor's appointment. It might be easier for your child to see—on paper—that the car needs to be washed Saturday, which conflicts with his attending the football game. Your job is to help him figure out that washing the car before leaving for the game is the only way to get everything done. (Don't fall for his creative suggestion that he wash the car *after* the game!)

Keeping Kids Stuff Organized

Another way to save your time—and your children's—is to set up their physical environment for easy clean-up and maintenance. Here's a checklist for a generic school-age child:

■ A twice-a-year clearing out.

IF YOU'RE SO INCLINED

Having a hard time getting your kids involved in organizing their rooms? Come up with a decorating theme that they can get enthusiastic about, and you might be surprised at the ideas they start suggesting. Girls might love all pink or all Barbie or butterflies, whereas little boys might want an "airplane room" or the latest Hollywood hero on their bedspread or curtains.

- Adequate workspace: a good-sized desk or table. (Even if they lie on the floor to do their homework, they'll need the flat working surface eventually.)

- Good lighting.

- Comfortable chair.

- Shelves or bookcases.

- CD or tape holders.

- Baskets for collecting little stuff.

- Hooks wherever possible; they'll increase the odds of getting clothes off the floor occasionally.

- A container in which to dump dirty laundry.

- Waste-paper baskets—big ones.

- Shelving in closets if they don't know how a hanger is used.

- An inexpensive (and washable) comforter covered by a duvet. They might even make their beds!

If this generic child is a teenager, you might not get much cooperation in organizing things or in keeping things tidy and clean in his room. You might make more progress if you let your teen make the decisions by asking her questions. How does she want to arrange her room, would she like to paint the walls, could she use more shelf space, does she need a shade to darken the room at night—all these inquiries are meant to entice her into participating in the process. Then, let her choose the duvet cover or bedspread, rug, or whatever additions the two of you decide might be useful or fun.

The Little Guys and What They Need

Tiny people need to be organized, too. You can make quick work of their rooms and belongings:

- Remove outgrown clothing often; they grow so fast that you can quickly end up with drawers filled with unusable clothes.

- Purge toys often. Hide some to pull out on rainy days.

- Use baskets for collections.

- Put sets of things, such as Legos, into plastic bins.

- Put puzzle pieces into Ziplock plastic bags; cut the picture of the puzzle off the top of the box and place it into the bag, too.

- Install a lot of sturdy hooks, at pint-size level, for pajamas, bridal veils, and cowboy hats.

- Use large mesh laundry bags to hold bulky toys; hang up on hooks.

Guess what? You can hope to achieve 50 percent my advice and be proud of yourself if you reach 15 percent. Rid yourself of idealized standards set by glossy magazine photos and TV programs.

Kids are meant to be kids. Perfectly tidy bedrooms don't make a whit of difference in their lives, but your sense of humor and appreciation of them will make a lasting impact.

GETTING GOING IN THE MORNINGS

If mornings are frantic around your house, you might want to adopt some useful habits so that everyone leaves

QUICK ⬤ *PAINLESS*

Keep a basket by the most-used door in the house. Advise everyone to deposit their library books, video rentals, and other outgoing items in the basket. Things to be returned will be—in a perfect world—together and ready to go when you are.

Figure out five breakfast menus and post them on a kitchen wall; you'll know what to prepare in advance the night before, and you'll hit the kitchen running in the morning without having to come up with creative menu ideas.

the house fed, with the most important items of clothing, and in fairly cheery spirits.

The Magic of the Night Before the Morning

Doing as much as possible the night before is the key to good mornings. Here's a checklist; pick a few to implement at your house every evening:

■ Be sure everyone's clothes are laid out for the next day. (Okay, maybe your spouse doesn't need this step.)

■ Make sure that everyone's backpacks are emptied to be sure that school notes have been signed, permission slips have been written, and forms have been filled out.

■ Make sure homework is completed and packed into the backpack.

■ See that everyone has money for lunch or the yearbook or the field trip.

■ If you make sack lunches, do as much as possible the night before.

■ Buy a coffee maker with a timer; prepare coffee the night before and wake up to fresh brewed Java.

■ Set the breakfast table after dinner!

■ Make the juice, pull bread out of the freezer, and grind the coffee; anything that can be done ahead should be.

■ If you have real winters, make a quick inventory of outerwear at night to be sure boots aren't sitting in puddles and that hats and mittens aren't sitting in soggy heaps.

- Pack your own briefcase or tote.
- The last thing you do while you're on your feet is glance in your planner to prepare for the next day.

Good Morning, Sunshine

If you've done some preparation the night before, mornings should work pretty well. Here are some ways to make things go quickly:

- Let the machine get the phone.
- Get yourself ready first if at all possible.
- Make your bed.
- Absolutely do not turn on TV.
- Have some tasks assigned: One finishes the lunches, one stirs the oatmeal, and everyone puts his dishes in the dishwasher.
- Put clocks in the bathrooms.
- If you're driving youngsters, alert them 15 minutes and then 5 minutes before you're due to leave.
- Set the clocks ahead by five minutes.
- Leave a few minutes early to allow for traffic delays.

Emergency Plans

The early morning phone call that will put any working parent right over the edge is the one from the day-care person who is sick and can't come to work. Be sure you have a backup plan (or two) for the days when you must

YOU'LL THANK YOURSELF LATER

Get up 15 minutes earlier if your mornings have been hectic; you'll get a lot done before everyone else starts moving about.

have your children looked after. The other parent, grand-parents, or a friend could all be possibilities. Check out what agencies are available—*before* you have the crisis.

SAVING KIDS' TREASURES

All that beautiful artwork that gets created every day by small children poses moral and storage dilemmas. How do you keep what's important? You might try several of these suggestions:

- Throw all school papers into a big basket or bin by the front door every day, and sort it once a month. You probably won't want to save more than about a third of what they've brought home. (If you're way over that, you need to let go.)

- Buy a large envelope for each child into which you put the items plucked to keep every month. At the end of the year, label the envelope with your child's grade and year, and stash it away some place.

- Use banker's boxes to collect incoming paper.

- If your child has an elaborate display or has created a bulky *objet d'art*, keep it for an appropriate amount of time. When everyone has tired of it, take a picture of your child standing by it (or holding it) and say goodbye to the item.

- Let your child pick out which drawings she wants to share with Grandma. Keep some large envelopes addressed to Grandma where you can store them before sending.

Getting Time on Your Side

	The Old Way	The Lazy Way
Making lunches in the morning	35 minutes	13 minutes
Number of last minute trips per month requested by your teenager	6	1
Hours spent alone with your spouse in a week	5	11
Finding your umbrella	Couldn't—had to buy a new one	30 seconds—it's on the way out the door
Making all the beds in the house	Never happened, but if it did, it would take 45 minutes	7 minutes (duvet covers are the secret!)
Hours spent at extracurricular activities per week	6	2

Chapter
twelve

Tip-Top Travel

Whether you're trekking to Tibet or entering the urban jungle of Manhattan, you still have to get from Point A to Point B in the least amount of time and in the most comfort possible. Once you get to your destination, you might need to function at a high level of productivity—a big enough challenge in the familiarity of your own office.

Frequent travelers often face a double workload: tending the office back home while accomplishing the work related to the trip. Add to the mix several time zones, luggage mishaps, strange beds, and computer blowups, and you've got the recipe for exhaustion.

The good news first: peace and quiet. Often, time spent waiting in airports, sitting on planes, trains, and automobiles, and resting during the gaps between appointments is the only uninterrupted time a lot of us get. It's up to us to use it well—and not just to work. Later in this chapter, I show you some ways to get the most out of your downtime travel time.

First, you need to back up from destinations to the planning stages. You remember the old adage about "One hour of planning will save you three hours of work," right? Long before you start packing, you should be getting the following things done:

- Schedule all your appointments well in advance.

- Consolidate as many meetings as possible geographically, for example, make sure everyone you need to see in NYC is going to be there while you are.

- If possible, fill in any long gaps by making appointments or scheduling meals with prospective new clients or customers.

- Be sure your hotel room has the space and equipment you need. At the very least, you need a desk with a phone close by.

- Ask ahead of time about plugging your modem into the phone jack in your room. Is there a separate jack for the modem, and is the hotel's telephone system compatible with your computer's needs?

- If you're jet-lagged and bounding out of bed at 5:00 a.m., take advantage of your morning energy by scheduling breakfast meetings in the city you're visiting.

- You'll undoubtedly start to crash in the late afternoon if you followed the preceding advice about breakfast meetings, so be good to yourself! Don't schedule any 4:00 p.m. appointments, and treat yourself to a nap before dinner!

- If you're going to be sending and shipping items from your hotel, ask whether it has a Federal Express or other similar pick-up service or system in place to accommodate you.

Great work! Your flight went great, you got some sleep on the plane, and you're ready for your meetings tomorrow. Take a walk to a nearby museum, or catch a movie you've wanted to see.

The Lazy Way

- If you're going to need this option, find a hotel with a small "business center" in it. It is a mini-office that offers computers, fax machines, and other business equipment and space in which to work.

- Be sure to check—enlist the help of your travel agent for this—that you have the necessary permits and visas for the countries you'll be visiting.

- Your travel agent should also be able to help you determine whether you need shots or vaccinations before you travel. Make sure you do this checking well in advance!

PLAN AND PACK A PECK OF PACKABLE PAPERWORK

That really says it all; you've got to spend some time up front planning what paper you need. Then, you've got to put it together—or separate it—so you can easily find what you need on the road—especially if you're carrying only one briefcase!

Using colored paper or plastic folders can be a good system for identifying different types of paperwork. On a plane, all your belongings might end up completely squashed under the seat in front of you, and you might need to be able to identify a piece of paper from a glance at its corner.

Here's what you might want to pack in your carry-on or briefcase to use on the plane:

- You'll probably pack different clients' documents separately so they're easily identified, accessible on the plane, and handy at your destination.

A COMPLETE WASTE OF TIME

The 3 Worst Things to Do When Traveling:

1. Schedule too many appointments in not enough time. (Finding your way around unfamiliar territory always takes a lot longer than finding appointments at home.)

2. Forget to allow enough sleep time. (Sleep-deprived equals unproductive.)

3. Fail to get an adequate room. (One where the only phone is by the bed, and the only work surface is the bathroom counter.)

- Cards, envelopes, and stamps make it easy to jot a note and get it out of the way.

- Take a few Federal Express envelopes.

- Bring along expense report forms or envelopes. It's *so* much easier to do your bookkeeping while on the road than tackling it when you get back home. There's always so much to do upon your return, and if you're like most of us, relying on your memory isn't a sure bet!

PARTNERING FOR PRODUCTIVITY

Those of you in small offices—without an assistant—need to efficiently cover for each other. Set up a system so that when you call the office, your partners have already gone through the mail and handled what they could, are ready to discuss the rest with you, have responded to those phone calls they could handle, and generally have kept the home fires burning. Expect to do the same for them when they're on the road.

Collecting as You Go

If you're away for any extended period, consider having someone ship your mail to you overnight; he should make copies of the important things for backup in case anything goes astray. By getting your mail while on the road, you can at least attempt to stay caught up and not face towering piles of paper when you get back to the office.

Some *Lazy Ways* to deal with the paperwork:

- Jot a reply at the bottom of a letter and fax it immediately from your hotel.

- Use a sticky note instructing your secretary what to do about each piece of correspondence, put it all into an envelope, and send it back to the office.

- Dictate responses to your correspondence on a small dictation machine (that you wisely packed in your carry-on!), pop the tape into an envelope, and send it to the office to be dealt with before your return.

- Compose your letters or work on a report on your laptop. Save to a floppy disk and send the disk to the office for processing.

Unloading as You Go

Don't feel you have to hang on to everything during your whole trip. Determine what can be sent back home mid-trip so you have less to carry and worry about.

Here's what you can wave goodbye to:

- Send a box with your already used presentation materials, binders, and manuals if you have to travel further and you won't need them.

- If you've had to travel to two climates, send the hot or cold clothes back that you won't be wearing again. At least send the bulky stuff, such as ski gear, top-coats, or even your wet-suit and rubber ducky. It pays to be prepared!

YOU'LL THANK YOURSELF LATER

If you check your bags, be sure that you have some necessities with you in your hand baggage—in case you end up in Sioux City and your luggage is sitting in Seattle. Medications, toiletries, and a change of underwear, along with non-replaceable documents or belongings, should be kept with you.

■ Stuff dirty shirts into a large envelope and send them home if you don't have time to wait for the hotel laundry. Be sure to warn the folks who are going to receive this package!

THE TELEPHONE ON THE RUN

Never more than when you're traveling do you need the telephone. What kinds of services and hardware you need can vary widely, depending upon where you're traveling, what equipment you already own, and how dependent on the telephone you really are.

Some folks do well with a minimum of telephone time: They've let people know where they are and how to get in touch with them if something urgent comes up. The rest of the time they're away, they can use email.

I use this system, augmented by checking my voice mail once or twice a day and answering any calls that can't wait. Callers who get my recorded message hear that I'm out of town and that they will hear from me upon my return. This lets you off the hook until you return, and you won't appear rude or unprofessional by not promptly responding to callers.

Some business travelers need constant contact with their office, clients, or support team. There are hundreds of options available in equipment and technology to keep you in touch. Your specific situation and requirements will dictate what you might need on the road. What you must consider when planning to communicate with others long distance is not just your needs, but also what kind of equipment and systems they are using:

QUICK ● PAINLESS

If key people know how to get in touch with you, and you absolutely don't need to check in with everyone while you're on the road, don't. Enjoy the freedom from the telephone while you can.

- If you're all on the same voice-mail system, that's an easy solution. You can send the same message to several people, forward messages you've received to others, and generally do a great job communicating within a closed loop.

- Cellular phones are an option, and they are essential if you're traveling by car frequently. They are getting cheaper every day. The actual telephones aren't hard to choose, but you'll need to do some research to get the best service provider and rates for your area to take into account the distance you generally travel.

- Pagers, unless you're a doctor or you're expecting calls of an extremely urgent nature, are one of my least favorite pieces of equipment from a time-management point of view. Pagers are great interrupters, notifying you each and every time a call comes through or a message is left for you. I believe that the kind of continual disruption that pagers invariably cause is highly counter-productive. If you're not doing anything else or you don't need to concentrate on what you are doing, and you feel the need to return every phone call within seconds, then the pager's for you. Otherwise, and at the risk of infuriating those addicted to them—I'd advise you to skip the pager option.

- You can always use the tried-and-true method; use your hotel room telephone with your calling card—the credit card issued by your long distance carrier.

QUICK ⬤ PAINLESS

If you've got an answering machine, you probably have a way to retrieve your messages with a remote access code. Learn how to use it before your trip: There is nothing more unnerving than "losing" messages while you're away.

An expensive alternative, generally, is using the hotel's phone and having the calls charged to your room. Most hotels add steep surcharges to all calls made from their rooms.

Some other things to think about and have arranged well before your trip:

- If you're taking your laptop overseas, be sure you have the adapters, cords, and plugs that will work in the countries you will be visiting. Your computer and modem manufacturers should be able to guide you.

- Be careful plugging your modem's telephone line into hotel wall jacks; they aren't always compatible and the wrong wiring system could play havoc with your computer.

- Consider a portable fax if you must send written documents frequently. Remember that you can fax directly from your laptop with the right software.

- Take along a surge protector for your equipment; you can find them for both domestic and international use.

A travel company called Magellan's seems to offer the answers to many a prayer about traveling electronic equipment. Among their offerings are modular telephone plug adapters for virtually any country in the world, which you can purchase separately or in a set of 34; a "patch cord kit," which contains everything you need, including a line tester to make telephone connections when there are no other options; power and phone adapters for every country; and surge protectors. They

YOU'LL THANK YOURSELF LATER

People reaching my voice mail are told the date I'm due back from a trip. I always tell them I'll be back a day later than I actually return. This is a great way to build in some catch-up and get-organized time after traveling.

also have an extensive line of suitcases of every fabrication, travel clocks, and other nifty travel accessories.

Magellan's also has real, live customer-service people to help with questions about what to take where, travel conditions around the globe, and technical help with electronic issues. Save yourself a lot of time and effort by speaking to them before you take off. See Appendix C, "Where to Find It," for how to reach Magellan's.

MAKING THE MOST OF DOWNTIME

As exhausting as it is, traveling sometimes gives you a few opportunities for quiet time that you might not get at home. While on a plane, at the airport, and even during a long cab ride, you can either get something done or one better: You can make every quiet moment count. Train yourself to relax, disengage, or be entertained. Here are some suggestions for how to keep yourself happy on a plane:

- Catch up on some reading.
- Listen to educational or motivational tapes.
- Watch the movie.
- Dictate into a small portable dictation machine.
- Listen to the music on the plane's sound system.
- Listen to an exciting thriller on tape.
- Write personal notes on cards you've brought along.
- Use your laptop.
- Think.
- Last but not least, *sleep!*

YOU'LL THANK YOURSELF LATER

I never have enough time at home to read all the magazine articles that look interesting, so I tear out the ones that I want to read and put them into a file folder for my next trip. This way, I get hours of pleasurable reading for my trip—without the bulk and weight of books and entire magazines.

More Pleasures

Once in your room, you might face long hours between appointments or until you need to catch your plane. Take your pick of pleasures to make the time go by and rejuvenate you:

- Take a nap.
- Order a nice meal from room service.
- Have a massage or beauty treatment.
- Visit the gym, work out, or sit in the sauna or hot tub.
- Rent a movie—or two!
- Pick out a slew of interesting-looking magazines from the newsstand and read them all.
- Take a nap.
- Take a long walk through the neighborhood.
- Get a hair-raising thriller from the gift shop and scare yourself reading.
- Watch Oprah!
- Take a nap.
- Venture out and buy the family presents.
- If you never have time to shop, this might be the opportunity.
- Visit a famous landmark or tourist trap or the local flea market—just because you never do things like that back home!
- If all else fails, take a nap.

IF YOU'RE SO INCLINED

I just discovered—after years of air travel that I never slept through—the benefits of a sleep mask. A dark, comfortable mask cuts out absolutely all the light in the cabin. (Even in a "dark" cabin, shadows and movements are somehow visible even with your eyes closed and can be distracting.) I can almost guarantee that the total blackness a mask provides will put you right to sleep.

Jeff Davidson, author of *The Complete Idiot's Guide to Managing Your Time*, has a couple of great suggestions for getting your sleep while on the road: Create "white noise" to drown out the kind of noises that keep you awake. Either use a machine designed for this purpose or turn on the room's thermostat fan. (Davidson recommends a device called a Sound Screen; see Appendix C, "Where to Find It.")

Davidson's second handy tip is to use earplugs. He recommends the industrial-strength quality plugs made by Cabot Safety Corporation called Noise Filters. See Appendix C, "Where to Find It," for how to get in touch with the Cabot Safety Corporation.

WHAT TO PACK AND WHAT TO WEAR

Pardon me for generalizing, but men seem to have mastered the art of packing better than women have. Of course, it doesn't hurt that they have only a few well-defined articles of clothing to consider, whereas women have infinite choices—and desires. The same dress for a week just doesn't cut it for any woman I know. Men don't seem to be bothered by the same pair of trousers and jacket every day while on the road, the monotony broken only by a change of shirt and socks. I deal with mostly women's issues here; read on for some good, *Lazy Way* tips.

In case you're wondering what your travel wardrobe has to do with time management, you probably don't have a problem with your packing. I know several women who hire help just to get them packed because

YOU'LL THANK YOURSELF LATER

Make your room wishes known when you make your reservations—not at check in. Confirm your requirements once again before you leave home. On arrival, you'll probably be tired and not up to a battle if they decline your request for a desk or fax machine, a non-smoking room, or a view. Have it all handled, to the extent that you can, beforehand.

they don't have a system that they can throw together in half an hour. Others report never feeling comfortable or pulled together while they're on the road because they don't have the right gear. Take the time to build a wardrobe system that needs only minor modifications for each trip.

Invest in good quality: Not only will good clothes pack and wear better, but also they'll look better longer. You need to look as great as you can as an antidote to all the discomforts and stress of travel.

Form and Function

Your first consideration is fabric that travels well. Second, pick out a few coordinated pieces that can be varied to change your look or fit in different situations.

Today's fabrics are truly miracle creations. Here are some fabrics that are especially wonderful for your travel wardrobe:

- Microfiber is the new, improved form of polyester and nothing like the polyester your mother wore.
- Tencel is a soft comfortable fabric and can be a good traveler.
- Good quality, lightweight wool, especially one mixed with a little synthetic, is durable and classy.
- Knits are always a good choice because they combat wrinkles beautifully.
- Anything blended with synthetics is likely to serve you well.

- Hands down, the most travel-friendly fabric (and my absolute top pick) is any fabric that's got a bit of Lycra spandex in it. Most often mixed with cotton or wool, this fiber transforms clothes into snap-back shape and stretchable comfort.

The Orvis Travel catalog is great for travel clothing, with a particularly generous offering of men's items. Their luggage selections look particularly well designed. See Appendix C, "Where to Find It," for information on Orvis.

Pick Any Color as Long as It's Black

After fabric, you need a base color. Black isn't really wonderful on everyone, but if you can wear it, great. Otherwise, you probably know your base color; navy, taupe, and even red are the most common and easy to put together with other basics. Any color will do as long as it's "yours." Use that one color and a couple of contrasting ones to put together your entire travel wardrobe. Here are just a few examples, if you're uninspired:

- Black as the base, with white and taupe as contrasts.
- Black with bright yellow and white.
- Black with natural, punctuated with a rich brown.
- Navy with the classic red and white choices.
- Navy with cream and rust to contrast.
- Taupe base, mixed with white and pale blue.
- Taupe with cream and black to contrast.

YOU'LL THANK YOURSELF LATER

Have your toiletry kit or cosmetic bags always packed and ready to go at a moment's notice. Use travel-size bottles and jars, found in drugstores and often provided by your favorite skin-care company. Be sure to refill everything as soon as you return home so it's ready for the next trip.

- Red base with black and cream.
- Red base with charcoal and white.
- Light gray with white and dark charcoal gray.

THE ESSENTIALS

After you've familiarized yourself with fabric choices and made a decision about your base and secondary colors, pick out the pieces to build your wardrobe. The most basic you'll want to consider are:

- Skirt
- Jacket
- Pants
- Sweaters
- Shells or t-shirts
- Blouse
- Coat

To this list, of course, you'll add, depending upon where you're going and what you're doing, workout clothes, a swimsuit, black tie clothes, or a wetsuit!

The skirt, jacket, and pants should be in your base color, but tops can be in different accent colors. Add dress-up or casual accessories to change the looks and function of your travel wardrobe.

Your coat should be warm enough for your destination (with a zip-out lining, perhaps) and made of one of the wonder synthetics currently on the market to combat wrinkling and resist rain. The darker the color, the better, of course—to camouflage dirt.

Travel Smith is a company with retail stores and a great catalog. They've done a great job figuring out the perfect travel wardrobe so that you don't have to spend time reinventing the wheel.

What they've dubbed "The Ready-for-Anything Travel Wardrobe" for women consists of a pair of pants, a skirt, a dress, a tunic, a cardigan, and a jacket. The versatility comes in the unique design of these garments. For example, the pants are convertible: The legs zip off to convert to a pair of shorts! The dress is their classic "Indispensable Black Travel Dress," (which also comes in dark navy), which can be dressed up with jewelry or dressed down with chunky shoes. It comes in long- and short-sleeved versions and below-the-calf or above-the-knee versions, and it is made from a modern absolutely-won't-wrinkle fabric.

Travel Smith also has a wide variety of other travel-friendly garments for both men and women and well-thought-out luggage offerings and accessories.

They have "Outfitting Advisors"; use them to help you pack appropriately for your destination. Remember: One of your new time-management techniques is to enlist the assistance of those who know more than you. Here's a perfect example of using that new skill!

A COMPLETE WASTE OF TIME

The 3 Worst Things to Pack for a Trip:

1. Glass bottles.

2. Too many clothes.

3. Different shoes for every outfit.

Getting Time on Your Side

	The Old Way	The Lazy Way
Time spent packing for a quick business trip	$3^{1}/_{2}$ hours	45 minutes
Time spent getting "caught up" after a trip	4 days	1 day
Letters written while out of town	None	11—all the important ones
Number of suitcases packed	2 huge ones	2 tiny ones
Hours of sleep you get on the plane	None	$4^{1}/_{2}$
Appointments seen in your three days in New York	4	8 (because you planned ahead!)

Chapter thirteen

Investigating Interruptions

Regardless of our differing work and home situations, all of us are victims of interruptions, generally from people intruding or the telephone ringing. Let's take a look at some ways to manage interruptions.

We all need other people in our business lives. But the people around us can nibble around the fringes of our day—if we let them—until there is no day left. Between the 15 minutes with Larry, the 20 minutes you were cornered by Alice, and two sessions with your boss—never mind the telephone interruptions—you can end up without much to show for the day. We all know the feelings of frustration that being busy and not productive brings, so let's figure out a way to balance it out.

Balance what, you ask? We need to strike a compromise between keeping the lines of communication open and controlling the amount of time we're available to others. We want to be available to those who need us for legitimate reasons, to move things along if we're the ones causing a bottleneck, or in case of a real emergency. At the same time, "legitimate reasons" can most often wait as long as discussing last night's ball game can. Here are some ways to keep the nonessential interruptions down to a minimum.

Keep in mind that it's not just the minutes the actual interruption requires that sabotages your time; the time it takes you to return to what you were doing when you were interrupted is the other half of the coin. It's difficult to change hats, shift your attention, and break your concentration several times a day, and it takes more time than you have to give!

AVOIDING INTERRUPTIONS IN THE FIRST PLACE

Obviously, the first line of attack is to lessen the frequency of interruptions. Study the types of interruptions you get and which people are the worst offenders. Seeing a pattern might give you a clue about how to proceed.

Plan for Your Interrupters

Perhaps a few key people need you often for your input, approval, or guidance. Have a frank discussion with them about their needs. Perhaps a regular meeting with them—or an additional meeting with them on a consistent basis—would cut down the interruptions. For example, Tom from your office might want to cut his Monday meeting with you but see you briefly—but consistently—on Tuesdays and Thursdays. This solution might not save

QUICK ● PAINLESS

Encourage people who want to walk in to send you an email instead. Explain that you'll get to it faster that way and that you'll call or email them back as soon as you get a chance.

the number of minutes you meet with Tom every week, but it would help get your—and Tom's—time under better control. Planning ahead will cut down on interruptions from Tom, might lessen his discomfort at having to interrupt you, and will undoubtedly save you the time you spend getting back on track after having been derailed.

Manage Others

This might take some firmness and self-discipline on your part, but if Tom should show up and interrupt you on Wednesday with a routine matter, you should respond that you'll be able to address his concerns at your usual meeting (tomorrow). Tom will need to be trained to write things down and save his questions and issues for your scheduled meetings whenever possible.

The First Line of Defense

If you're lucky enough to have an assistant, then you have a great ally in protecting your time, but you also need to protect yourself from your assistant! Frequent visits from anyone—even a highly competent helper—can greatly reduce your productivity. Be sure that you have agreed upon a system that works for both of you.

Conflict can arise from your need to be left undisturbed versus your assistant's needs to see you often in order to proceed. Set up a schedule whereby you both get what you need from each other. Obviously, flexibility—yours, that is—is crucial. Assistants will always need to interrupt you on occasion to alert you to the inevitable emergencies and urgent matters.

YOU'LL THANK YOURSELF LATER

Make an effort to use some preventative measures at the office and you'll see a reduction in daily disturbances.

Your assistant has another important role: that of screening your unscheduled visitors. A simple, "Mrs. Miller is in a meeting right now. May I make an appointment for you for later in the week?" could potentially save you many productive hours. Be sure you spend an adequate amount of time explaining and training your assistant how to handle drop-in visitors.

A good assistant will also—if the visitor has urgent business—have the authority to make a last-minute appointment at a time of day that works for you. Appropriate, in this case, might mean right before or after another appointment. Your assistant should be trained not to book anything for you in the middle of an unbroken period of time in which you just might get some work accomplished. Again, training is key here.

Another technique for cutting down on interruptions is to simply shut your door—assuming you have one. If that doesn't mean "not available" in your office, go one better: Put a sign on the door stating, "I'll be available at 4:00 p.m." or "Got a deadline; please leave a voice-mail message." or "Please make an appointment with Mary; I'll be available tomorrow."

Beat 'Em to the Punch

I'd be willing to bet that 80 percent of the interruptions you get are from people who might have been able to handle the situation themselves, especially if they're looking for things. Think ahead. If you're trying to get something done at home, be sure the kids have enough supplies, juice, or pencils to complete their homework or snack time. At the office, save yourself time in the long run by being sure that everyone has the rules, the information, or the equipment to do what they need to do—without traipsing into your office.

Another good reason for being unavailable is that if you leave it to others to figure out a solution, they often do—without you. That is precisely what you often want your co-workers to do! It's amazing what your staff might get accomplished on its own. Many questions and who knows how much hand-holding can be avoided simply because things had to get done—with or without you. Remove yourself from the picture and you might end up with more self-sufficient co-workers and more time on your hands.

AND IF NONE OF THOSE BRILLIANT IDEAS WORK?

Okay, the barrier has been broken, and you've got Sam at your door just needing "a quick word with you." All the lines of defense have been penetrated. How do you proceed?

What you say and how you behave will immediately encourage the visitor or communicate your unavailability. It's important that you respond appropriately so that others quickly learn that coming to you unannounced is not a great idea. You can be nice. You can be polite. And you can take control. If you're constantly interrupted, it sounds like you might benefit from practicing some of the following responses:

QUICK ● PAINLESS

Want a simple trick to discourage drop-in visitors? Keep the chairs in your office occupied. If they can't sit right down, they'll be out the door soon!

- Body language—yours!—can be a subtle, but strong indicator of your responsiveness. Not looking up from your desk, or glancing up only briefly, tells the interloper that you are not available.

- Don't make eye contact; that will just show that you've been distracted.

- Stand up rather than gesture to your visitor to sit down. Stand up and stay that way while you're talking. It's just not comfy, and your conversation will end sooner. Your standing up also communicates that this discussion needs to be brief.

- Have one chair in your office and keep it occupied with stuff—your jacket, briefcase, or books—signaling that the chair is unavailable. This is one time when clutter is useful!

- Politely ask your visitor what he or she needs. How you respond verbally can tell your interrupter volumes. Your tone of voice can be sharp, short, or mildly irritated.

- "Does this need to be handled now? If so, tell me exactly what I can help you with, and I'll tell you when I'm available to work on it."

- Depending upon the answer, you can respond with, "I can spend five minutes with you right now. Is that enough, or do we need to make an appointment later in the week?"

- If what they need requires more than a brief encounter, explain "Sallie, I think your problem is going to take more time than I have right now. Can we hold off on this until I get back from my trip?"

- As you near your deadline, politely say something like, "Jack, before we wrap this up, give me a quick rundown on what you've done about this situation." Glance at the clock or your watch while you say this. You've just verbally and visually signaled that his time is about up.

- If you need to respond to the interrupter's request, tell him you'll meet him in his office in five minutes. You'll maintain control of the situation by being the one who can leave. It's like driving your own car to a party; your stay will be unfettered by other people's schedules.

Assistant to the Rescue Again

Another way to put your assistant to work for you is to plan some kind of signal for him to interrupt you—a good interruption! Your signal might be "If Mrs. Jones calls, please put her through; I've got to talk to her today." Ten minutes later, the call from Mrs. Jones will miraculously arrive, and you'll graciously excuse yourself to your visitor.

Visiting Hours

Establish hours in which you are available and hours during which you're not to be disturbed. Again, structuring your time—before someone else does—is the key to controlling your day. It just may happen that some problems will be resolve themselves before your "visiting hours."

YOU'LL THANK YOURSELF LATER

On the outgoing message of your machine or voice mail, ask the caller to indicate what time of day is the best time to return the call. If your assistant takes messages, train him to ask for the same information. It should save a lot of time spent playing telephone tag.

Congratulations! You've tamed the telephone! Treat yourself to a new CD to listen to while you get stuff done!

The Lazy Way

THE TERROR OF THE TELEPHONE

As great an invention as the telephone may be, nothing has done more to fill our days and interrupt the silences we need in our lives. Not only does the telephone alert us audibly, but also it seems to carry its own brand of urgency. It appears that one of the hardest things to do is simply let telephones ring. Learning that one skill might win you back a significant amount of time. Here are some ways you might find helpful to control the telephone:

- You need backup in some form: an assistant, voice mail, or an answering machine.

- Ask your assistant to screen your calls, getting as much information as possible from the caller. It might turn out that your assistant can handle the call, and you'll never even know about it. If not, the more you know about who called and why, the easier you will be able to prioritize and prepare for getting back to him.

- Let the machine pick it up. A machine often has the advantage of allowing you to screen your calls. This gives you the opportunity to take only those calls that are essential and let the others record for later. I'm amazed at how often people hang up without leaving a message. It certainly indicates that a lot of calls are either unimportant or couldn't have been terribly urgent.

- Another advantage to leaving a message (on either an answering machine or voice mail) is that if the caller simply needs to relay information, she can do that—without the small talk preceding and ending most conversations.

- Let voice mail do its job. Don't pick up the phone. Collect your messages a few times a day.

- If you're rehearsing for this afternoon's presentation or concentrating on writing the conclusion of your report, keep the ringer turned off. A ringing telephone—even an unanswered one—is disruptive and can effectively break your train of thought.

Returning Phone Calls

Retrieve your messages a few times a day. You might return the most important ones immediately. Then, return the rest in batches, when you're taking a break, sipping a cup of coffee, between tasks, or before leaving for the day. Don't get too comfortable; you still want to get through your conversations as quickly as possible.

Just as you do with your in-person interrupters, it sometimes helps to alert the person you're calling that your conversation with them is drawing to a close. Here are some verbal alerts you can use to communicate that you intend to end the conversation soon:

- "Jean, before we hang up, let me ask you one more thing...."

- "I don't want to keep you any longer...."

- "Joyce, I've got to get to a meeting now, so was there anything else we needed to discuss?"

- "I've got to let you get back to work...."

QUICK ⬮ PAINLESS

Do not respond, "Hi, Barbara. How are you?" That open question can enter you into the caller's personal and social realm. Instead, get straight to the point by asking something like, "Hi, Barbara. What can I do for you today?" This technique makes it clear that you want to get right down to business and should help you avoid a lot of chit-chat.

More Sneaky Tricks

Here are a few more ideas to help you avoid interrupters, find some quiet space, and keep yourself productive:

- Get out of your office, and hide in the conference room to work peacefully.

- Leave the office altogether, and do your writing project at the library or a quiet corner of a coffee house.

- Stay at home one day, and catch up on your reading, phone calls, and email.

- Arrange your office so you're not staring at the open door, inviting a conversation; keeping your head averted and aimed toward the work at hand is a good trick.

- Position your desk so that you don't look up—even inadvertently—into a hallway or corridor. Anyone wandering around might catch your eye—and your attention.

- If repositioning furniture doesn't work, or you have to share an office with a chatty type, perhaps a screen to divide the room or block off vision into your workspace would be helpful.

Home Work—Keeping Interruptions to a Minimum

If you're a homemaker or you have a home-based business, you face special challenges to combat interruptions if working at home is a new situation for you, your spouse, children, or roommates. They might assume that you are more available than you used to be when you left for the office every day. You might even have less time than you used to if you're just starting a business—and that can be hard for your housemates to fathom. It's one thing not to talk to you while you're away from home, but having you right down the hall might be too tempting to resist.

Outsiders might also pose a problem. Friends might pop by for a quick chat—something they'd never do if you were downtown at "the office." Having you handy by the telephone could work to your detriment as well. Some folks will always tend to think that if you're at home, you're on leisure time.

If you've been in a home office situation for a while, you probably consider yourself extremely lucky, but you've probably also figured out that you need to be firm with friends and family and have a fairly high degree of self-discipline to withstand the temptations to goof off.

Here are some tricks you might want to add to your arsenal:

- Establish your work hours. Anyone who calls for a social chat or drops by to "see how you're doing" needs to be told that you can play, but after hours only! Get used to communicating clearly that you can't chat right now but will get back to your visitor or caller after 5 (or 6 or 7…).

- You might sometimes have to leave the house and hide out at the library or coffee shop.

IF YOU'RE SO
INCLINED

Scope out a few secret hiding places for those days when the home office is just too hectic.

- Keep office doors closed to children if possible.

- Start a children's—and possibly, spouse's—training program early. They need to be taught to respect your work space and time.

- Get a separate telephone line for business purposes. Give it only to those you do business with. During work hours, let the answering machine take care of the home line.

Kids and the Home Office: How to Keep Everyone Happy

Children could prove to be the biggest issue you have to handle while working at home. There is no perfect solution, but consider these ways of minimizing intrusions:

- You owe it to yourself and your children to physically remove yourself as far as possible from the center of the action. A separate room that you can close off is essential.

- Get as much done as possible while they're at school (if you've got school-age kids).

- Younger children might understand the system of setting a timer—for a half hour, an hour, or more or whatever they can comprehend. When time's up, you can spend a little time with them, have a snack together, or play on the computer for a few minutes.

- Get kids used to the sight of a closed door.

- Make things as soundproof as possible. Kids need to make noise, and there's nothing less professional

than the rumble they make while you're on a business call.

Remember that you're working in your kid's home; they need to feel safe and happy there, just as you need to feel productive. Traditionally, too, children are a little unclear on the concept of making a living and what it is you're actually doing in that room over there. Be patient, and move further down the hall.

PROCRASTINATION

To the subject of procrastination: It might not be something that impacts you, but if it is, keep reading. This is one tough subject, folks. We're going to study the issue pretty carefully, and take a look at how to get off our duffs and stop putting off dreaded—or boring or too hard or silly—chores.

> "The best time to plant a tree is 20 years ago. The second best time is right now."
> —Chinese proverb

The Chinese got it right. Nike got it right: "Just Do It." It's a brilliant thought that will probably endure for many more centuries because it goes to the heart of the matter—the human tendency to put off the inevitable.

Some procrastination is normal and sometimes necessary. Sometimes, it can even work to your advantage. How many times have you put off doing something only to discover that it didn't need to be done, that someone had changed his mind, or that the problem resolved itself? There are times when procrastinating will save you

QUICK 🔲 *PAINLESS*

Repeat after me: "The best time is NOW!"

time. I truly believe that letting some things "gel" a bit—such as ideas for a proposal or how to best handle disciplining an employee, for example—will produce better results because your subconscious has done some problem solving for you.

Mostly, procrastinating will cause you pain, lost time, mental anguish, worry, sometimes seriously irking other people left to wait for you, guilt, and stress. It really seems hardly worth procrastinating; the price can just be too high!

What keeps us from digging in and just getting to work? To ask the question another way—what will help us "just do it?" It seems that some conditions to be met will make it much easier for you to jump right in. Mostly, you need to be clear on the concept. If you're currently procrastinating about something, answer the following questions about the task. The answers might lead you to an explanation of your inactivity:

- Do you know what exactly needs to happen?
- What does the end result look like?
- How will you feel when the job is finished?
- What impact will the completed chore have on your life?
- What will the impact be on others?
- Do you need help?
- Can someone else do it?
- Are you qualified to do it?
- Are you lazy?
- Is there a way to make it fun?

A COMPLETE WASTE OF TIME

The 3 Worst Chores to Procrastinate:

1. The project your boss asked you to do.
2. Medical and dental appointments.
3. Getting your car in for service.

- Do you have to do it at all?

- Is the job consistent with your own beliefs and values?

- Is the job just going to take too long?

- Is the job illegal or morally questionable?

- Is there a power struggle going on? Sometimes, we initiate some kind of passive-aggressive war by not doing anything.

- Are you afraid of failure?

- Is your energy at a low ebb? If it is, find out why. Are you ill, not taking care of yourself physically, depressed, or sleep-deprived? Seek professional help and get to the root of the problem. Keeping your mind and body in good shape will definitely make your life flow more easily.

This list should considerably help you get rid of the job by determining whether it really has to be done, by helping you decide to delegate it, or by figuring out exactly how to do it. It might also make you see more clearly that you shouldn't do the job for one of several reasons.

More Marvelous Moves

There are some other ways to make your to-do list more inviting—or at least a little less daunting. Try these techniques:

- Reward yourself. Actually treat yourself to some form of "gold star" like your teacher gave you in first grade.

QUICK ⬤ PAINLESS

Sometimes, even when you're feeling overwhelmed and you don't know where to start, start anywhere! Once you get going, you'll not only feel better, but also it will probably become apparent when each step should be done.

- Do the hardest first. Every day, do a hard job first and get it out of the way.

- Make it fun.

- Break it down into small steps. Having a clear picture in your mind of each step should get you to the starting gate a lot faster.

- Plan out each step of the project on paper. Somehow, writing the step down makes it much more likely that it will happen.

- Set a date for completion and write it in your planner.

- Block out times in your planner to complete each step of the project.

- Make a verbal commitment to those who will be impacted—your boss, your spouse, or your children.

- Begin!

Sometimes, it isn't the chore that you're putting off; it's a decision. Not making a decision can really screw up the works because nothing can happen until you've figured out what's supposed to happen. Get through the decision-making process more easily:

- Talk things over with a trusted colleague, friend, or family member.

- Write down the pros and cons on the same piece of paper.

- Listen to your gut.

- Take a break from thinking about it; walk around the block or come back to it tomorrow.

Because your projects will be a series of small tasks, make a note to yourself which step is next when you stop working for the day. That way, you won't have to spend time figuring out where you left off when you resume work the next time.

- Don't over-analyze; spend a reasonable amount of time collecting the most pertinent data.

- Accept responsibility, regardless of the outcome.

- Use the process of elimination if you have several choices. In a three-step process, eliminate the least likely alternatives in one step. During a second round, eliminate the next least likely. Third, make your decision from the remaining few choices.

- Don't demand perfection from yourself. Some personality types get so caught up in the details and minutiae of a project. Don't let the little stuff take control. Do the best you can, accept it as a good thing, and move on.

- Just make a decision—even if it's the wrong one. Even if you've made a mistake, rarely is it going to have life-changing impact.

Congratulations! You've cut down your interruptions and helped your colleagues set up appointments with you instead of just dropping in. Treat yourself to lunch at your favorite restaurant.

The Lazy Way

Getting Time on Your Side

	The Old Way	The Lazy Way
Average number of interruptions per work day	13	6
Hours spent planning your club's annual fund-raising event	15 hours	$4^1/_2$ hours
Number of times you confer with your assistant per day	12 times	4 times
Percentage of appointments you arrive to late	42 percent	3 percent
How long you put off getting your tax information together	'til April 9th	'til February 1
How much time you spend on the telephone	4 hours/day	$2^1/_2$ hours/day

The Art of Saying "No" and Doing Nothing

All the time-management books in the world aren't going to benefit you unless you learn and make a practice of many of the techniques I've covered so far that are designed to help you stay in control of your time. The enemy surrounds us: our co-workers in the next cubicle, the telephone, our adorable children, our buddies dropping by, the boss with yet another urgent project.

One of your last lessons in this book concerns the art of saying "no." Without this skill, you are going to be a passive victim, so develop this art, and you will stay on your own track, focused on your goals, and you'll get a heck of a lot more done. The irony is that the more you say "no," the more you will accomplish!

Saying "yes" when you mean "no" is one of the worst underminers of your priorities and schedule. Following are some tricks to get you in the habit of using the word "no" often and well. Having learned to decline, I discuss the ways

you can say "yes" to relaxing, withdrawing, finding solitude—and doing nothing at all.

THE "Y" WORD

The price extracted for too much to do—because we said "yes"—can be enormous. Here are some consequences of the Y-word:

- Being chronically overbooked is likely to make you awfully grumpy as well as increase your stress level. Sooner or later, your health will be impacted, not to mention your relationships.

- Remember the "important but not urgent" time quadrant (the all-important Quadrant II)? Too many things going on means the urgent quadrants are probably running your life. If that's the case, you can bet on the fact that your Quadrant II activities probably are not getting done. And you're probably not getting a lot accomplished.

- Other people are going to be negatively impacted by your having too much to do. Children and spouses, for example, are often given short shrift when you're consumed with work. Co-workers and projects get left waiting for you to do your part. Subordinates don't get the training and supervision they need because you've run out of time. I don't need to tell you that feelings get hurt—and that running around always feeling guilty is not fun.

- The quality of the work you accomplish might suffer. Racing through a project might bring results that are just not up to your—or others'—high standards. What's the point of low-level performance? You're not aiming for perfection here, but you must have enough time to do a decent job.

- You can't squeeze in one more important task between many other important projects and expect that you can produce great results from each and every one of them. Get help, quit, change something—cut back!

- Even worse, you might agree to do something and never get it done. This will not only disappoint others and damage your credibility, but also you won't feel good about yourself. Don't set yourself up for failure. We don't need to lower our own self-esteem; we have others who can do that for us!

- Downtime gets lost. Think about how long you can expect to keep a frantic pace without rest or relaxation. Sooner or later, without a doubt, you *will* burn out.

- Being really busy makes some of us feel really important. Unfortunately, it doesn't work that way. You might tend to look instead like a doofus—someone who has not handled her time wisely, who is disorganized, and who is definitely not in control of her destiny!

Why is "no" so hard to say for some people? Here are my musings on the subject. Do any of these descriptions fit your profile?

YOU'LL THANK YOURSELF LATER

Take a second to sit back and honestly evaluate yourself; this means accepting the good and the bad. When you hit spots where you feel that you could be doing better, think about your obstacles. Odds are pretty good that a lack of time management and saying no are the main culprits.

- We are programmed to be "nice." Nice people don't refuse other people.
- We want to be liked. Maybe people won't like us if we say "no."
- We respect—or fear—authority.
- We think we have to provide a good explanation for our "no."
- Being busy makes us feel important and valued and feeds our egos.
- Being hectic and frantic might impress others with how valuable and in demand we are.
- We *want* to say "yes."
- We don't know how to say "no."

If any of these motivations (or rationalizations) sound like they might apply to you, take a closer look. Wanting to be liked and to be nice are often the fallout of low self-esteem. You might need to remind yourself that you are a valuable employee and a fine person—*without* having to take on more than you can handle or take on something you're not prepared for or qualified to accomplish. Having your life chewed up by others' priorities is not smart. And it's certainly not the way to boost your self-esteem. Taking charge and standing your ground is how to start feeling good about yourself!

You're not always required to have an explanation for your "no." A superior in a work situation might need to be enlightened about what else you're up to, and the

IF YOU'RE SO INCLINED

How many times do you find yourself saying this: "Well, okay, but just this once." If you say that more than you say "I'd love to, but I have way too much on my desk right now," then you probably need to learn how to say "no." As a matter of fact, maybe you should read this twice!

two of you might need a discussion about priorities, but the majority of your "nos" needn't be defended. Again, you need to value yourself, your time, and your decisions—without apology. No one else will if you don't.

YOU CAN'T DO IT ALL

If you keep saying "yes" because you are truly interested and willing to participate, but find yourself racing to keep up or always falling behind, you have some choices to make. Remember: You can do anything; you just can't do everything. You simply must decide how you are going to spend the time you have. Really learn that in spite of what the magazines tell you, you can't do it all—regardless of how much you'd like to.

One way you can help yourself to say "no" is to return to your list of long-term goals and your action plans. The most important question to ask yourself when making a decision about whether to do something is, "Does what you're being asked to do fit into your plan?" If you have a clear sense of your priorities, it'll be a lot easier to answer that question and a lot harder to stray too far from your path.

If you simply don't know how to say "no," or must re-train your mouth's habit of saying "yes," keep reading. I've got some handy suggestions for you in the pages ahead, and I provide some good reasons and a few techniques to better handle those tough demands on your time.

YOU'LL THANK YOURSELF LATER

Think before you answer! A few extra seconds can mean the difference between staying on track or getting distracted from the "plan."

Delegate as much as you possibly can. It does mean giving up some control, but which would you rather lose, a little control or your mind? See Chapter 4 for creative ideas on delegation.

The Cost of "Maybe"

In a few situations, "maybe" can be the appropriate answer to a request of your time. Generally, however, "maybe" just delays the inevitable. Like diving into a cold pool—say "no" fast, and get it over with. Here are some examples of when "maybe" works:

- If you've been asked to take on a job, "maybe" might be the right answer while you negotiate sharing the job with someone.

- While someone figures out whether there's enough money in the budget to hire help for you, "maybe" works.

- "Maybe" might work if you'd like to consult with your family. You might want their input to determine whether your partner (or kids) might be interested in joining you in a project or activity.

Most of the time, however, the word "maybe" just generates interest on a bad debt. "Maybe" delays the decision-making process and requires you to worry about how to say no, weigh the alternatives, and spend more time and energy than a simple "no" would have done. Not only do you suffer from delaying tactics, but also "maybe" holds up everyone else impacted by your decision.

"Maybe" is especially dangerous if you wait too long to say it. You might feel so guilty by then, or have held up the requester so long that there are no other options—that you *have* to say "yes" at that point. By default or with a surplus of guilt are definitely not the ways you want to reach decisions regarding how to spend your time.

Decisions, Decisions

Knowledge is power, as we all know. This is never more true than in the decision-making process. The more you know about what's being asked of you, the higher the odds you'll be able to make the right decision. Here's what you can do to get all the facts and figures and determine the real impact a project will have on your time:

- Listen carefully to the requesters. You can validate the requests and leave the asker, if not with "yes," at least the knowledge that you really heard him.

- Get a job description of any position you're being asked to hold.

- Ask for an estimate of how much time the project or position is likely to involve.

- Assume that the requester will make light of the negatives.

- Do some research: Ask others who have been involved or held the position what it really entails.

- Listen "between the lines." If you're told that serving as president can get a little hectic during the holiday fund-raisers, it might mean that you won't see your family during the month of December.

- Always, always ask yourself whether it fits into your master plan.

QUICK 🔲 PAINLESS

Don't let your ego fall for the line that "You're the only one who can do the job." Sorry, but that's rarely the case.

Two good rules:

1. It's always okay to say "no" right away.

2. It's never okay to say "yes" right away. Think it over for 24 hours as you would a big purchase. There's often no "buyer's remorse" clause to protect you once you've agreed to committing your time.

HOW TO SAY "NO"

You might not be well versed in saying "no" if you're reading this chapter. If you think of yourself as less than adept at staring down the enemy, you might find the following scripts helpful:

- "George, I'm sorry but the timing's wrong. I'd like to help organize the office party, but until I finish this year's financials, I can't take on any more."

- "Kathy, I'd love to take you shopping. But I promised the kids that I would bake cookies with them on Saturday afternoon."

- "No, John, I won't be able to do the newsletter next year. Sorry."

FADE TO BLACK

Not everything you do can be abruptly terminated. You might have commitments to fulfill and projects to finish. At least write down a plan: what activities are going to be weeded out or cut back. Phase out as quickly as you can.

YOU'LL THANK YOURSELF LATER

When someone gives you an estimate of the time required by a project or position, double it. *Then*, make your decision.

"No, But..."

Saying "no" doesn't have to be a negative. You can be gracious, firm, and direct, keeping your main priorities in line, and be helpful to the asker. You can recommend alternatives, solve problems together, delegate to someone else, or offer suggestions. Here are some examples:

- To George, described previously, you might offer to ask your secretary to help.

- With Kathy, I might add, "But let's make a date for the following Saturday!"

- To John: "Let's brainstorm and see who we might ask to take over next year."

- Say "no" first, and then offer something less in return. If you decline the presidency of the club but still want to make a contribution, you could offer to take the treasurer's position.

- If you're asked to chair a committee, decline—but offer to work on the committee if that interests you.

- If someone asks for a report with figures, ask whether they'd be satisfied with only the numbers. (Let her do the report.)

- Say "no" this time, but commit to hosting the next meeting—but only if you really want and intend to host the meeting. Don't use this as a ruse to delay the inevitable.

- Make a deal. "Karen, if you'll pick up my child at school, I'll have time to edit your letter."

Great job! You resigned as your club vice president. With the free time you gained, do absolutely nothing at all!

The Lazy Way

Another way to set boundaries for yourself is to establish times or days that are off-limits for work or outside activities (assuming you have a choice in the matter). Where you have freedom to decide, make decisions about your time. It will be a lot easier to say "no" if you have "rules"—even if you made them up.

Okay, you've made a conscious choice about an activity and taken it on, signed on the dotted line, and committed to it. Now, all you have to remember is that there are several paths to the same destination. Choose *The Lazy Way*! Here are some examples and some solutions that might work for you:

You've been asked to bake cookies for your child's classroom party. The hard way is to bake those suckers yourself. *The Lazy Way* is to go out and buy some nice cookies.

You are asked to send out letters for your organization. Instead of writing personal letters separately, *The Lazy Way* reader will write one letter, make a copy for each recipient, and scribble a personal line on the bottom of each one. Then, hire a kid to fold, stuff, seal, and stamp the envelopes and get them to the post office.

You've offered to help in your child's classroom once a week. Change the time from afternoon to morning and get up earlier. You'll be finished with your commitment early in the day and have the rest of the day to be productive.

Doing your club's correspondence can be a huge chore. Keep up with it, when appropriate, by email.

You've agreed to put together your organization's newsletter. Here's how you can share the job: Rather than track down all contributors yourself, enlist a helper to collect all the material and see that it gets to you on time. Then, all you have to do is put together the parts of the newsletter later.

NOTHIN' DOIN'

What prompted you to read this book? Were you feeling frantic? Overwhelmed? Out of control? Grumpy? Longing for respite? Whatever the feelings, I hope by now that you have adopted some new time-management techniques that have improved your life.

All new habits take practice. Give yourself time to learn new routines. Nothing as significant as some of the organizational and time-management issues I've covered in this book can be changed overnight.

Short-term quick fixes are helpful. Long-term, life-changing new habits are the way to a calmer life. We're going to look at some fundamental changes you might want to make and ways to rethink what you're doing that's keeping you so busy.

The Balancing Act

The need for balance in your life is not to be ignored. Putting off taking some time for yourself or your family will sooner or later impact your life. The results of neglect will show up somewhere—in your poor health, a disgruntled spouse, an acting-out teenager, or lost productivity.

Isn't the point of time management to gain more time—*not* to gain more time to do more of what's been making you crazy? Isn't the point to change something—

YOU'LL THANK YOURSELF LATER

Guilt can work effectively to rope you into something you don't want to be roped into. You can't fix the world. Don't make other peoples' problems your problems.

not just cram more of the same into the same 24-hour period? Only you can make those changes; only you can make the choices that will improve the quality of your life. What you do with your new-found time will have lasting effects on you, everyone around you, and your work.

I've seen people so caught up in the work "habit" that they've forgotten who they are and what they love outside of work. It may have been so long since you've had a chance to sit down and think about what's important to you, you might want to use the following reminder list. It's just suggestions of non–work-related activities that you may have forgotten belong in a balanced life.

Which of these ring a bell? Was there a time in your life, before you got so caught up in the rat race, that you loved to do something? Is there something you always wanted to try? Is there something you need to do for your health—physical *or* mental? Try these ideas on for size; see what appeals to you:

- Play a musical instrument.
- Hike.
- Read trashy novels.
- Read real literature.
- Learn horseback riding.
- Take a drawing class.
- Finish your needlework pillow you started in 1966.
- Write that novel you have inside you.

- Go to a spiritual retreat.
- Build a computer.
- Go to AA.
- Write a poem.
- Sit on the beach.
- Join a gym.
- Learn to cook.
- Sew a dress.
- Build a bookcase.
- Go swimming every morning.
- Take a bath.
- Work on a campaign.
- Watch movies.
- Write in your journal.
- Garden.
- Build a better dog house.
- Learn photography.
- Sit in the park.
- Meditate.
- Tutor kids at the local school.
- Make your own paper.
- Trek the Himalayas.
- Recycle.
- Build shelves somewhere.
- Volunteer.

YOU'LL THANK YOURSELF LATER

Think of a time when you were truly content, when there were no regrets and frustrations that kept you up at night. Recall what you were doing at that point in your life. What decisions did you make that put you in that state of mind? You were probably taking better care of yourself. Staying on top of things means staying on top of what you need for yourself.

- Daydream.
- Go camping.
- Play with your children.
- Get season tickets—for whatever.
- Do nothing.

Whew. Absolutely overwhelming, yes? Doesn't it seem the impossible dream? But you can—you *must*—bring into your life those things that will keep you healthy, lower your stress, engage your imagination, clear your head, invite discovery, open your senses, keep your perspective, nurture your relationships, and enrich your life.

You have a limited amount of time on the planet. How you choose to spend your time will define your life. Starting today, you can start writing the rest of your story in terms you'd like to see applied to your life. You have the ability to choose powerful over panicked, fun over frantic, peaceful instead of pressured, creative over crazy, and healthy instead of hectic.

SLOWLY, SLOWLY, SIMPLIFY, SIMPLIFY

Simplifying your life is probably the one activity that will buy you more time than anything. The less you have, the less you have to worry about or take care of, the less space you will need, the less you'll need to insure, the fewer resources you will need, the less time you will have to spend accumulating resources, and the less time you will have to spend keeping track of things in your already over-taxed brain. Pare things down.

Simplification means more than cleaning out your kitchen cupboards or file drawers. Real simplification means clearing out your mind as well as your physical environment. Life-changing simplification is about making lifestyle changes. They can be anything from miniscule tweaks to enormously significant changes.

Following is a list of some areas in your life that might be somewhat simplified. Some will apply to you; some will be completely inappropriate. The point is to start thinking of your life in a more stripped-down—or "downsized"—form.

- Rid your home of everything that is not functional or beautiful.
- Get a smaller home.
- Consider whether you could survive with fewer vehicles.
- Choose one or two extracurricular, volunteer, or hobby activities; let the rest go.
- Keep one set of dishes. Keep one set of utensils. Don't get rid of the "fine China." Use it everyday and enjoy it!
- Edit your wardrobe so that it fits into half your closet.
- Cut up your credit cards. Pay cash.
- Get rid of the television.
- Consolidate investments.
- Stop all but the most informative or entertaining subscriptions.

IF YOU'RE SO
INCLINED

Try yoga. The combined practices of breathing, stretching, and major mental concentration will have you leaving class as a limber and energized wet noodle.

- Become unavailable to people who don't enhance your life.
- Don't even glance at the catalogs that arrive in the mail.
- Eat fresh food.
- Buy only the books you love. Read the library's copy first, and then buy it only if you feel you must have it.
- Work at home.
- Get organized.
- Walk whenever you can.
- Keep only one checking account.

Simplifying your life does not mean ending up with impoverished results. On the contrary! Your life will be richer—in the things that really matter.

INNER AND OUTER WORK

In addition to getting yourself organized and developing time-management techniques, there are other resources to use—mostly originating from your own body—to slow you down. None of these are quick fixes. All of them require a certain discipline to begin or master. But there is something to be said for traditional practices that have brought serenity for centuries:

- **Breathing.** Inhaling and exhaling oxygenates every cell in your body, relaxes your muscles, works as a painkiller, and makes a contribution to the earth's need for carbon dioxide. Practice slow, deep breathing. It will calm you.

- **Meditation.** It's the art of being still and clearing the clutter from your mind: doing nothing but just *being*. A simple, difficult practice that takes repetition, meditation helps time stand still. Meditation can provide answers that bubble up out of the quiet, making themselves known in the stillness. Once you quiet the brain's cacophony, wisdom has a chance to reach you.

- **Exercise.** Try some good, sweaty, heart-pumping effort. Get your muscles warm and working, your lungs giving their all, your heart being used as it was meant to be used, and the feel-good endorphins blasting!

- **Sleep.** The healer, sleep lets the body repair itself and the mind work out its own conflicts, dilemmas, and flights of imagination.

- **Stretch.** Make like a cat. Unkink your muscles and joints, the targets of all the stressors coming your way. Lengthen yourself; grow yourself longer and leaner. And breathe.

Congratulations! You've made it this far. You're even sitting down. You have made a conscious decision to read. You're in control—at least for the moment. Draw yourself a hot bath and stay in there until it isn't hot any more.

The Lazy Way

Getting Time on Your Side

	The Old Way	The Lazy Way
Number of times you said "no" in a week	1	4
Hours out of 48 you spend with family in a weekend	25	48
Hours exercised in a week	2	6
Number of nights spent in meetings	3 to 4	0 to 1
Number of times per week your kids complained about your not being available	6	2
Hours of downtime you take in a week	5	15

More Lazy Stuff

A

How to Get Someone Else to Do It

We talked about delegating in Chapter 4 and the necessity of carefully weighing the time-saving benefits of hiring someone to help you against the cost of doing so. Remember that more than time is often at stake—your very sanity could be on the line!

Finding good help can be a real challenge, and you may have to make a few mistakes before you figure out how it's done. The important thing is to keep trying, be flexible and keep your mind open to unconventional solutions.

And if the budget is a problem, don't forget the age-old benefits of bartering—trade what you're great at with someone who'll do what they do best on your behalf!

LEAVE NO STONE UNTURNED

Be sure you don't overlook possibly under-utilized members of your community when looking for people to help you. Some population groups you may not have thought about are:

- Retirees—they are often experienced in the working or homemaking worlds and may be looking for a part-time way to supplement their income. I'd look amongst them for help with everything from babysitting to bookkeeping to gardening to filing.

If you live near a retirement community, a mobile home park, independent living facility or have a senior center nearby, post a large notice on their bulletin boards and see if you don't get a response.

■ Don't forget kids!—from your seven-year-old who can be hired to set the table every night, to the teen next door who loves to drive your junk to the dump in his new truck, to the college student who needs office experience. A high school girl or boy could take your children out for a walk every afternoon while you start preparing dinner. Washing the car, folding the laundry, setting up your computer or hooking you up to the internet, yard work, window washing, running errands, grocery shopping—all these are activities that can be delegated. And mature youngsters can be that extra pair of hands or legs at the office to answer the phone, stock the shelves, do clean up or deliver packages.

Most high schools and colleges have someone on staff to coordinate work programs for their students. Give them a call and get yourself some help while providing that experience every young person needs. Or ask if there's a bulletin board on campus where you can post a notice.

A library's bulletin board is also a good place to advertise your need for help—both students and seniors often frequent the library.

■ Family members, of course, can be another resource for help. Most of us have been known to hire our kids to do specific, extra chores. If you don't have your own stable of children, try nearby nephews and nieces, cousins and other relatives. You might be surprised to find out what their talents are beyond showing up at family gatherings! Ask.

- We all usually ask our friends for referrals of people they've used to perform various tasks, but it might never occur to us to hire or trade services with our buddies. Nothing ventured, nothing gained!

Below are some suggestions as to where to look to find specific kinds of help. Good luck!

Accountants/Bookkeepers

Generally you'll find what you need by asking for referrals from friends and family. You might also try your local Small Business Development organization for suggestions, as well as your Chamber of Commerce. Be sure to interview anyone you're considering hiring and ask for (and check!) references.

Closets

California Closets. 800/274-6754

The Great American Closet Company. 800/305-8555.

Poliform. State-of-the-art closet designers who use the finest materials and all the bells and whistles your closet could ask for. 212/421-1220.

Ask local contractors if they've had experience in closet design or refurbishing. (Ask to see pictures of their work).

Cooks

If you've struck out with all other options, try calling around to caterers to see if someone would like a part-time gig cooking a few meals a week for you or your family.

Estate Organizer

Professional organizers often do this type of work. You might also try accountants' and attorneys' offices for suggestions. Stockbrokers may have come across someone performing this work, too.

Insurance Adjuster

Contact the National Association of Public Insurance Adjusters in Herndon, Virginia. 703/709-8254.

Medical Claims Adjusters

The Alliance of Claims Assistance Professionals. 630/588-1260 or www.claims.org. Someone in your doctor's office may also know someone appropriate.

Moving Coordinator

Seek out a professional organizer or ask local moving companies and real estate firms for referrals.

Photograph Albums

Creative Memories. 888/227.6748.

Professional Organizers

NAPO (National Association of Professional Organizers) can be found by logging on to www.napo.net or by calling 512/206-0151. To find a local organizer in your community, look in the yellow pages under "Organizing Services & Systems-Household & Business."

Tutors

If you're looking for your children ask their teachers and administrators for referrals. The local high school may know of students who could tutor younger kids. Talk to a community college for possibilities of a tutor for your high school student—or yourself.

Wardrobe Consultants

Look for personal shoppers at department stores, ask friends and co-workers, or look in the yellow pages under "Image Consultants or "Wardrobe Consultants." Your best bet may be a well-dressed friend who is willing to spend some time with you.

B

If You Really Want More, Read These

Here's a list of really great books (if I do say so myself) to help you along in your quest for time-management improvements. Some are business oriented; others are geared to household and family issues. You'll find them all online. Better yet, order them from your local, independent bookseller.

Just remember—you're not going to get this perfect. Enjoy the fine-tuning you can do in your life, and delight in every small step forward.

A Complete Waste of Time; Tales and Tips About Getting More Done, Mark Ellwood. Pace Productivity, 1997.

Clean Your House the Lazy Way, Barbara H. Durham. Alpha Books, 1998.

Cook Your Meals the Lazy Way, Sharon Bowers. Alpha Books, 1998.

How to Get Control of Your Time and Your Life, Alan Lakein. Signet, 1973.

More Time for Sex; The Organizing Guide for Busy Couples, Harriet Schechter and Vicki T. Gibbs. Dutton Books/Penguin, 1995.

Organized to be the Best! Susan Silver. Adams-Hall Publishing, 1991.

Organize Your Stuff the Lazy Way, Toni Ahlgren. Alpha Books, 1999.

Organizing Options; Solutions from Professional Organizers (A compilation of tips from the San Francisco Bay Area Chapter of the National Association of Professional Organizers, 1994.) Available from SFBA NAPO, 1952 Union Street, #721, San Francisco, CA 94123.

Prioritize Organize—The Art of Getting It Done, Jonathan and Susan Clark. National Press Publications, 1992.

Taming the Paper Tiger: Organizing the Paper in Your Life, Barbara Hemphill. Kiplinger Books, 1992.

The Art of Doing Nothing; Simple Ways to Make Time for Yourself, Véronique Vienne. Clarkson Potter Publishers, 1998.

The Complete Idiot's Guide to Managing Your Time, Second Edition, Jeff Davidson. Alpha Books, 1999.

The 80/20 Principle: The Secret of Achieving More with Less, Richard Kock. Currency/Doubleday, 1998.

The Overwhelmed Person's Guide to Time Management, Ronni Eisenberg with Kate Kelly. Plume/Penguin Books, 1997.

The 7 Habits of Highly Effective People, Stephen R. Covey. Fireside/Simon & Schuster, 1989.

30 Days to a Simpler Life, Connie Cox and Cris Evatt. Plume, 1998.

Time Management for Unmanageable People, Ann McGee-Cooper. Bantam Books, 1994.

Where to Find It

I've told you about all the great products that are out there solely to help you organize your time; now, here's where I tell you where you can find them.

GENERAL ORGANIZING PRODUCTS

Basically, it comes to this: Whatever your needs are, someone else has probably already designed an answer to your organizing predicament:

- **Abbott Office Systems.** This manufacturer offers reference-material organizers for desktop or wall mounting. Send for their brochure. Call 800-631-2233, or fax them at 732-938-4419.

- **Get Organized.** They provide a catalog offering general organizing goodies. Call 800-803-9400 or visit getorginc.com.

- **Hold Everything.** They have stores and a catalog, so don't leave the house if you don't have to! Call 800-421-2264.

- **Lillian Vernon.** Ask for the "Neat Ideas for an Organized Life" brochure. Call 800-285-5555.

- **Lizell.** Here's yet another catalog of office supplies: big and small, bookcases to baskets. Call 800-718-8808 or visit lizell.com.

- **Target Stores.** This is a nationwide chain, and it is a pretty safe bet. Check your Yellow Pages for a location near you.

- **Racor.** It sells a line of heavy-duty hooks and racks for big, bulky, or outdoor equipment (such as hooks to hang bicycles in the garage). Call 800-783-7725.

- **Reliable Home Office.** Find everything for the office including furniture. Call 800-869-6000.

- **Rubbermaid.** This is the name you love for good-quality plastic boxes, bins, and virtually every kind of storage container. They are available in stores nationwide, or you can write for the home products or industrial products catalogs: Rubbermaid, Inc., 1147 Akron Road, Wooster, OH 44691-6000. Call 800-362-1000.

- **Solutions.** Here's a catalog of handy household items and tools. Call 800-342-9988.

- **The Container Store.** Stores and a catalog offer kitchen and pantry products, shelving systems (including the Swedish Elfa wire-basket system), and closet components. Call 800-733-3532.

SPECIALISTS

You know exactly what you think you need but have no idea where to find something like that? I've compiled a list of people to call for those specific needs; trust me, these people will help!

Clothes

Being organized also means looking organized; you'll never make the right impression and get a chance to show how organized you are if you look like you couldn't care less. Start with the basics.

Reach the Doncaster Collection by calling 800-669-3662 or visiting www.doncaster.com. The people at Doncaster will direct you to a consultant in your area.

Closets

Conquer those closets! Whether you've got too much stuff, not enough space, or a combination of the two, try these companies out and take control:

- **Closet Dimensions.** Call 800-743-6961 or visit closetdimensions.com.
- **California Closets.** Call 800-336-9174 or visit calclosets.com.

Direct Mail

A Web site that claims to remove you from both direct mail and telemarketing lists is populardemand.com. I recently requested that they remove me from telephone lists, so I can't report the success rate. But, hey—it can't hurt!

Ergonomic Equipment

Doing well starts with being well, so treat your bones to ergonomically designed furniture. You'll thank yourself later.

Call or fax for catalogs from these companies:

- **Fox Bay Industries, Inc.** Call 800-874-8527.
- **Kensington Microware Limited** in San Mateo, CA. Call 800-535-4242 or fax 650-572-9675; visit kensington.com.
- **North Coast Medical, Inc.** Ergonomic Products Division, San Jose, CA. Call 800-277-6826 or fax 408-283-1950. Visit the Web site at ncmedical.com.
- **Workrite Ergonomics** in Novato, CA. Call 415-884-2311, fax 800-930-8989, or visit the Web site wrea.com.

Food

If you were to add up all the time you've spent running to the store, you'd realize people spend an inordinate amount of waking time getting the same stuff every week. Let someone else do the running around, and you can keep your kitchen stocked without losing your mind:

- **Homeruns** provides its own catalog of foods—just about everything you'd find in your local supermarket—and will bring it right to your kitchen. You can phone, fax, or email your order as late as midnight the night before you need the delivery. Call at 800-882-RUNS (7867), or find them online at www.homeruns.com.

- **Horizon Foods,** found in several states, is a working mother's dream. Good-quality, prepared entrees are delivered frozen to your door. Call 888-EASYFOOD or go online at www.horizonfood.com.

- **NetGrocer** resides online at www5.netgrocer.com. You can order virtually anything you'd find in a huge grocery store, and get it Fed Ex'd to your door within two to four business days. The service is especially cost-effective if you live on the East Coast, and shipping is downright inexpensive for the northeastern states.

- **PeaPod** is one of the first online grocery shopping services, with delivery zones in several cities. Submit your grocery list, and have it delivered to your door—seven days a week. Check it out on www.peapod.com.

Medical Claims Adjusters

If you're in the middle of a health crisis of any kind, whether it's an illness or accident, you don't have to slog through the confusing paperwork by yourself. Especially at a time like this, it pays to call in someone who knows the ropes.

Call the **Alliance of Claims Assistance Professionals** at 630-588-1260 or log on to www.claims.org.

Planners and Datebooks

You need a place to put your plan, right? Take advantage of the companies that make your plan their business:

- **At-A-Glance.** These products appear at many office supply and chain stores. To look at (but not buy) their offerings, check out www.at-a-glance.com. Call 800-365-YEAR (9327) if you can't find what you're looking for.

- **Day Runner.** Look in your local office supply store, call 800-232-9786, or find them on the Net at www.dayrunner.com.

- **Day-Timers, Inc.** Call 800-225-5005, fax 800-452-7398, or visit day-timer.com.

- **FranklinCovey.** Call 800-975-1776 or visit franklincovey.com.

- **Levenger.** Find the Circa line of notebooks, including planners. Call 800-544-0880 or visit levenger.com.

- **Spiegel Appointment Books.** Find these at Office Depot or Ogle Publishing, whom you call at 503-625-1890 or email at info@oglepub.com.

Office Supplies

Any efficient office, whether it's in a house or a high-rise, runs smoothly because it's well stocked with the little things that make life easier. Take a page out of every big businesses' book, and make sure you've got all the odds and ends you need—but not the ones you'd never use, of course—to keep things moving.

Quill has a fast, efficient mail-order service and offers virtually every office-supply item you could possibly want. It carries name brands as well as its own less expensive lines, and shipment is speedy. Call 800-789-1331 or visit quillcorp.com.

The following stores appear in just about every town across the country; check your Yellow Pages!

- **Staples**
- **Office Depot**
- **Office Max**

Organizers

At a loss about where to start? Don't let it get to you. Even getting organized can be easy. If you're really feeling snowed under, enlist a professional organizer to get you going:

- Look in the Yellow Pages for "Organizing Services and Systems—Household and Business."
- **NAPO (National Association of Professional Organizers).** Log on to napo.net, or look in your Yellow Pages under "Organizing Services and Systems—Household and Business."

Photographs

We love taking those pictures to preserve the fleeting moments in our lives, but then what do we do with them? Take some time to preserve and organize all those pictures your family has taken over the years; after all, your loved ones deserve better treatment than molding away in a box, don't they?

- **Creative Memories.** Call to attend a cut-and-paste session, where you'll learn the basics of archiving photographs and you can purchase good-quality albums and journaling supplies. Call 800-341-5275.
- **Exposures.** Purchase products for organizing photos—albums, frames, boxes, and cabinets. Call 800-222-4947.

- **Light Impressions**. Find supplies for archiving photographs, negatives, and slides. Call 800-828-6216.

Stationery

Appearance counts! Whether you run a small company from your basement, you are part of a large corporation, or you help organize community events, it's important to put your best face and paper forward. People will remember an elegant piece of stationery much better than they will a note scrawled on a piece of legal paper:

- **American Stationery Company.** This is my favorite source for attractive, handy personalized items. Order postcards and address labels to make quick work of routine correspondence. Call 800-822-2577.

- **Hallmark.** This catalog offers several lines of business-oriented greeting cards, attractively designed to make it easy to stay in touch with business contacts and build upon established relationships. Hallmark Business Expressions, MD #580, P.O. Box 419291, Kansas City, MO 64141-6291, Call 800-404-0081 or log on to www.hbe.hallmark.com.

- **Quill.** Among its offerings of every office supply imaginable, you can get quick letterhead and envelopes at reasonable prices from Quill. Call 800/789-1331 or visit quillcorp.com.

- **Tiffany & Company.** Among the best. What more can I say? Call 800-526-0649.

Telephone Headsets

If you spend any amount of time on the phone at all—and honestly, who doesn't?—then treat yourself to one of these little gizmos. Look, ma—No hands!

Hello Direct has a slew of headset, teleconferencing, and telephone options. Call 800-444-3556 for a catalog or visit hello-direct.com.

Travel

Whether you need luggage or a sleeping mask, these companies can help you make your next trip a breeze.

Easy on the Ears!

It's time to make your traveling tranquil, so if you're interested in some of these products, give the companies a call:

- **Noise Filter Earplugs.** Cabot Safety Corporation, 5457 W. 79th Street, Indianapolis, IN 46268. Call 317-872-6666.
- **Sound Screen White Noise Device.** Marpac Corporation, P.O. Box 3098, Wilmington, NC 28406-0098. Fax 919-763-4219.

The Right Stuff

Big or small, these companies have great stuff in stock to help you on your travels:

- **Magellan's Travel Outfitters.** Call 800-962-4943, fax 800-962-4940, or visit magellans.com.
- **Orvis Travel Catalog.** Call 800-541-3541 or fax 540-343-7053.
- **TravelSmith Catalog.** Call 800-950-1600.

D

It's Time for Your Reward

Once You've Done This...

Set up your planner.

Purged your filing system.

Emptied your closets of
everything not worn in a year.

Made a two-week dinner menu plan.

Billed your clients on time.

Written down your long-term
and short-term goals.

Delegated at the office by
hiring a payroll service.

Delegated two chores at home.

Said "no" when asked to
be treasurer of your club.

Made time to go skiing.

Reward Yourself...

Schedule a massage.

Get a beautiful plant for the office.

Buy yourself a new pair of shoes.

Go out to dinner; the plan starts
tomorrow night!

Take a leisurely walk to deposit
those checks.

Take a long weekend with your
significant other.

Give yourself a raise—or ask for one.

Take the kids to the movies.

Buy yourself a thrilling mystery novel.

That was your reward!

Where to Find What You're Looking For

Now you can do these tasks, too!

The Lazy Way

Starting to think there are a few more of life's little tasks that you've been putting off? Don't worry—we've got you covered. Take a look at all of *The Lazy Way* books available. Just imagine—you can do almost anything *The Lazy Way!*

Handle Your Money The Lazy Way
By Sarah Young Fisher and Carol Turkington
0-02-862632-X

Build Your Financial Future The Lazy Way
By Terry Meany
0-02-862648-6

Cut Your Spending The Lazy Way
By Leslie Haggin
0-02-863002-5

Have Fun with Your Kids The Lazy Way
By Marilee Lebon
0-02-863166-8

Keep Your Kids Busy The Lazy Way
By Barbara Nielsen and Patrick Wallace
0-02-863013-0

Feed Your Kids Right The Lazy Way
By Virginia Van Vynckt
0-02-863001-7

*All Lazy Way books are just $12.95!

additional titles on the back!

Learn French The Lazy Way
By Christophe Desmaison
0-02-863011-4

Learn German The Lazy Way
By Amy Kardel
0-02-863165-X

Learn Italian The Lazy Way
By Gabrielle Euvino
0-02-863014-9

Learn Spanish The Lazy Way
By Steven R. Hawson
0-02-862650-8

Shed Some Pounds The Lazy Way
By Annette Cain and Becky Cortopassi-Carlson
0-02-862999-X

Get in Shape The Lazy Way
By Annette Cain
0-02-863010-6

Clean Your House The Lazy Way
By Barbara H. Durham
0-02-862649-4

Care for Your Home The Lazy Way
By Terry Meany
0-02-862646-X

Redecorate Your Home The Lazy Way
By Rebecca Jerdee
0-02-863163-3

Stop Aging The Lazy Way
By Judy Myers, Ph.D.
0-02-862793-8

Learn to Sew The Lazy Way
By Lydia Wills
0-02-863167-6

Train Your Dog The Lazy Way
By Andrea Arden
0-87605180-8

Organize Your Stuff The Lazy Way
By Toni Ahlgren
0-02-863000-9

Shop Online The Lazy Way
By Richard Seltzer
0-02-863173-0

Take Care of Your Car The Lazy Way
By Michael Kennedy and Carol Turkington
0-02-862647-8

Get a Better Job The Lazy Way
By Susan Ireland
0-02-863399-7

Cook Your Meals The Lazy Way
By Sharon Bowers
0-02-862644-3

Cooking Vegetarian The Lazy Way
By Barbara Grunes
0-02-863158-7

Master the Grill The Lazy Way
By Pamela Rice Hahn and Keith Giddeon
0-02-863157-9